# Culture Gap

T0161385

Published by New Star Books

*Other books in the Transmontanus series*

# Culture Gap

TOWARDS A NEW WORLD IN THE YALAKOM VALLEY

*Judith Plant*

**TRANSMONTANUS / NEW STAR BOOKS** VANCOUVER

*For all nine of my grandchildren and my new great-granddaughter, and for all children everywhere; may these stories help you to find real love.*

*Guardian of the trail to Camelsfoot, a rock art painting by Juan Coyote.*

PHOTOGRAPH: JOANNE KIMMEL.

# The Trail

**Summer 2013**

It is a hot, late-July day. Many people are making the trek up to Camelsfoot, our Shangri-La, to say goodbye to Susan, our dear friend and communard who passed away in the spring. Susan was Fred Brown's perfect partner. Fred was our mentor.

Camelsfoot is northwest of Lillooet in the interior mountains of British Columbia. During the gold rush someone had the crazy idea that camels would do well here as pack animals, and actually brought them into this dry landscape more aptly suited to the resident mountain goats. Today, some will travel in 4x4 trucks up the steep mountain pass — a seven-mile journey that takes an hour to drive it's so treacherous.

While I have travelled that pass many times, I drove it myself only once, during a storm. It was dark and rain pounded the deeply rutted road; rocks seemed to be falling all around us. We were returning too late from a trip to town. Eleanor, a fellow communard, with three year-old Robin on her lap, guided me through every inch of the many switchbacks as I carefully backed up and went forward, again and again, to avoid the sloughing sides that would have sent us end-for-end hundreds of feet down the slope.

3

Decades later, on this sunny day in July, I avoid the pass and take the trail instead, an hour-and-a half walk uphill across scree slopes and gorges, alongside the fast-moving creek.

Susan's celebration of life will bring together many of the original communards, and friends both young and old, to honour and celebrate her remarkable life. Robin, the now-grown daughter of Eleanor and Van, organized the event — a sign of how important a figure Susan was to her, and to many young people. Van Andruss, who wrote Fred's biography[*] and who was Fred's closest friend on the commune besides Susan, will no doubt take a leadership role as we gather together to share our memories. It's not easy to get to "the Foot" and not all of the old group have been able to make the trek, but about half the original members are here: Alice, Kelly, Glen, Kip and me, some of our children, also now grown. Many others who Fred and Susan influenced have also made the journey to join in this celebration of Susan's well-lived life.

I am hiking the trail with my eldest daughter Julie, her husband Sandy, and their two teenage sons, Ben and Thomas. Kip, my husband of thirty-four years, my son Will and his young family, and Julie's youngest child, Hannah, make the journey over the pass in Will's 4x4. Kip has been dealing with a degenerative neurological disease for seven years and sadly he is now mostly in a wheelchair. It's a show of both his fortitude and his love for these people that he has made the great effort to leave the comforts of home and make the long trip from Gabriola Island, where we have lived for over twenty-four years. I know he wouldn't have missed this event for anything.

Hiking the trail is a moving experience for me in the bright morning sun. Julie and I have walked it many times before, decades ago. Then we carried heavy packs loaded with oranges, mail, and

---

* A Compass and a Chart: The Life of Fred Brown, Philosopher and Mountaineer. Lillooet: Lived Experience Press, 2012.

*Judith hiking the trail into Camelsfoot with Willie and Shannon, 1983.*

other delights from town. We've even carried plywood, but that's another story. In the winter our steps were secured by ice creepers or even crampons buckled over our felt pac boots. There's little snow in these mountains but lots of ice and frozen ground from cold, dry winters. The trail is impossible to travel safely in these conditions without this ice climbing gear on your feet. In the summer, of course, it's hiking boots.

The boys can hardly contain themselves. There's something thrilling about walking a trail with a destination, an end-in-view, with every step bringing a fresh experience along the way. Fred taught us to set the right pace by putting the slowest person in a group of hikers in the lead. I take the lead with the boys, who often charge ahead and run back to us, doing double time without

*Bird's-eye views of the trail (above) and the meadow (facing).*
PHOTOGRAPHER
UNKNOWN

a care. Returning to Camelsfoot almost thirty years later with my grandchildren and Julie and Sandy, to a place and time in my life of such enormous significance, makes every step precious.

When we get to "Culture Gap" I try to explain the significance of the place and its name. Early on Fred named many of the hills and mountains around Camelsfoot, melding into the landscape our endless conversations about who we were and what we were doing here. Culture Gap is a steep gorge, with soft scree that has taken a few loose-footed walkers down its free-falling slope. Crossing the Gap moves the traveller from the old world to the new world — at least that's how we communards thought of it. It took courage to reach the other side, the new world. And it's dangerous. You know as soon as you see it that it could take your life if you're not completely paying attention. Julie rode a horse up this trail once, through the Gap, along the scree slope. Now that's bravery for you. Most people navigate the soft, vanishing trail with well-placed boots, hanging on to a rope tied to a tree high up the slope — absolutely thrilling for the boys.

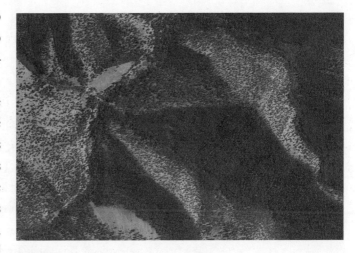

Is it really different on the other side? I think so. In the valley below, Ponderosa pines dominate the landscape; as we gain altitude and cross the Gap, majestic Douglas firs stand like welcoming giants, so far avoiding the dreaded logging that increasingly threatens much of this territory. The mill in town, after all, is only twenty-nine kilometres away. Everywhere the scent of juniper lingers.

Once across we head straight for the cold rushing water of the creek. In the "old days" we always kept a cup hooked on a branch. This hot July day we all splash our faces and drink our fill of the most pristine, delicious water in the world. Crossing the makeshift bridge we are now on the other side of the creek, in the "parklands." It is different. The roar of the creek subsides, the bunch grasses whisper in the wind and tickle our bare legs, the massive firs offer stability and calmness. The slope is gentler. We're getting close.

The five of us are quiet as we walk the last third of the trail. We bathe in the atmosphere of the place. By now we have shed a lot of our nervousness and excitement and are just putting one foot in front of the other, enjoying every minute. Soon we come to the meadow, the sloping several acres that have made hay for horses and goats over the years but now lie fallow, to the delight of the mule deer. Up we go. Others have already arrived; we can see their vehicles parked in the birch grove up ahead. It's not an easy journey to make, by truck or foot. But we are here . . . now.

I'm looking out the window of the large kitchen addition built several years ago with Susan's inheritance. Across the alleyway is the old kitchen, the cookshack. People are milling about. I see Sandy, my son Will, old friends, children. Robin and others have made a great effort to open up the buildings for this event. The place is alive today, but deeply empty at the same time. I have to shake my head to keep it real. No one lives here any more.

As I walk through the building to the original cabin, memories come in big emotional gulps. The cabin was the heart of the commune in many ways. We had two pianos, shelves of music, oriental carpets, all remnants from our respective lives elsewhere. The walls were lined from floor to ceiling with an amazing library. Rare books, encyclopedias (at least two sets), any and every book by John Dewey and George Herbert Mead. All the classics in both literature and social change theory. Even the children's corner was rich in books.

Big ideas were had in this cabin. Decades ago inside these rough-hewn walls, we worked and re-worked our story of a new world that would nurture people and place, a new culture that would be resilient in the face of the crumbling old world. We talked a lot about evolution, about human beings as social creatures who need culture to make sense of the world, and how this has been lost to us. And just in case we should ever get carried away with our own self-importance and think ourselves the centre of the universe, we had replicated the solar system in iridescent papers on the ceiling, placing us and the Earth in context.

I sit down in the now empty space and try to play the dusty old Heintzman . . . it's hopelessly out of tune. While I hear people's voices from the new kitchen, there is not the same atmosphere of purpose that once permeated the place and I am overwhelmed by waves of sorrow, for the loss of our friends but also for the end of our ideals, for what was so hopeful and promising when we were much younger and, perhaps, braver. Yes, we have lost Susan. But maybe we have lost a great deal more.

We communards had gathered together in the cabin every

morning with our second coffees to discuss the day. We eschewed the conventional idea that the new world would emerge in the hallowed halls of parliaments or congresses. No, we told ourselves, what was needed was a culture, a living, breathing framework of love, support, and belonging. The creation of a new world would emerge from the stuff of everyday life. So, working backwards, we'd first decide who would be cooking dinner, then discuss the children's activities, and finally, who would get time at their desk that day. In the late afternoon, we'd gather for another coffee klatch. We were looking for inspiration and often found it in each other.

The end of the day was my favourite time: finally putting our feet up in a (mostly) tidied-up space with dinner percolating on the cookstove, the woodstoves roaring. We were deep into the mountains and it was very cold in winter. There were piles of felt pac boots at the door — some people even kept them on. No one complained of this, of course. That would have created an "issue" out of something minor.

All of this comes back to me as I wander through the now-empty

*Some of "the folks" gathered at the top of the meadow.*
FROM LEFT: *Bonnie Mae, Scott, Alannah, Shannon, Julie, Willie (in shadow), Kelly, Alice, Van, Eleanor (with Robin), Sheila, Judith, Kip.*
PHOTOGRAPHER UNKNOWN

9

*The Cosmic Office*
*back then — a*
*favourite writer's*
*hideaway.*

cabin. We believed so wholeheartedly in what we were doing, and I can feel the loss even today, thirty years later. When things fall apart, as I have since discovered they invariably do, we each take our turn breaking down. When our inspired life took a turn for the worse I was no exception. A few dusty books remain on the shelves and the old RSF stove still dominates the room, but there is no commune anymore, no budding new world. The life is gone. Dead. So it seems.

But today, decades after the collapse of the commune, we are here to remember Susan and inevitably to honour Fred as well. The place is full of family and friends. Robin and the others have made a huge effort to make this gathering happen. The food and drink alone are more than significant. Later we will feast on salmon; Koochi, native elder and dear friend of many, will grill fresh sockeye on the fire already started outside the cabin.

Around noon about sixty of us make the trek, one way or another, up the hill to the grove of aspens just below the clearing we called the Cosmic Office, a now-dilapidated shack once used as a quiet

*Fred and Susan with
their dog Teddy.*

writing space. With water bottles and cushions in hand and chairs
for some, people find their spots and a circle grows naturally.

Everyone speaks in turn. Susan's love of horticulture comes up
over and over again, as does people's gratitude for her parenting
guidance. I remember her mostly as a person who was never afraid
to "step outside the box" — even if only to have popcorn for dinner! "She was the most generous person I ever met" is heard many
times. It takes over five hours in the hot sun but no one leaves the
circle. Not even the children. Not even my grandchildren who
knew Susan only by reputation. They are enraptured by the event,

by the deep meaning in each person's contribution. Even if the listener does not understand the spoken words, the feelings are so authentic and heartfelt that understanding comes from a deeper place. So it is for the children, and all of us, who are riveted.

Several strong men, including Thomas, Will, and Camilche, Robin's Cuban husband, take turns with the pick axe. Finally, the hole is dug. Susan's ashes are laid down beside the spot where Fred's ashes were placed twenty years ago. A cairn is built by careful placement of special rocks. Then it is done. Fred and Susan are together again in the Philosophers' Grove.

Back at the cookshack, we open bottles of beer and wine, spread out the fabulous food, and celebrate. Not for long for Julie, Sandy, Thomas, Ben and me, though. We are taking the trail down today and have to keep our wits about us and an eye on the setting sun.

Years ago I walked down this trail in the light of the full moon, by myself. Or I thought I was by myself, until I sensed that I was being watched. Cougars live in these hills and I could feel one nearby. I had seen signs earlier. But I had to get down the trail that night, there was no turning back. I can still recall how light my feet felt, how sharp my senses were, as I made my way in record time!

I don't want to leave everyone, but I know the trail will be stunning this evening after such an event. Back down we go. Through the meadow, into the parklands, across Culture Gap, down to the foot of the trail, leaving behind the celebrating people, and the shadows of the inspiration of the community life that surrounded Susan and Fred and many of us.

Darkness draws near as we find our vehicle. The soft summer air is full of love and sadness. We head back to my son's place — he and his family live next door to Eleanor and Van, dear friends and fellow communards, and across the valley from Robin and her family. I pour myself a scotch and sit down in the cool evening air to reflect on the day and the days gone by.

# ONE

# We Take the Plunge
# (and the Trail)

**Summer 1982**

It was late August and still very hot. I was hiking alone up the trail to Camelsfoot with a heavy pack on my back, choosing to walk rather than drive. I'd done this trail before, but this was the first time that I was "going home." While the hike in is only a little over three miles, it is uphill all the way. But the trail was well maintained and even though there were spots where I would have to use both hands and feet, I knew that if I was careful, I would arrive safely. I had just quit smoking cigarettes so my lungs were straining with each step. The discomfort of the climb was overshadowed by the excitement of the adventure. The trail was so stunningly beautiful, and this was a moment to myself.

Kip was driving the mountain pass on the seven-mile rough mountain road. The children were with him. Julie was hardly a child at sixteen, but Shannon and Willie were, at ages thirteen and ten. Willie was beside himself with joy, but Shannon was angry.

» » »

Camelsfoot, a huge acreage nestled in a mountain valley and completely surrounded by Crown land, had once been an outdoor

13

school but, as Van would later describe it in *A Compass and A Chart*, they had left little behind: "a dilapidated cookshack, a lopsided barn, a foundation for a cabin, and several outlying cabins crudely built. There was an undeveloped garden a quarter mile downstream from our domestic centre that we used for the first few summers. It was the perfect place to throw off your clothes and enjoy the sun. . . ."

In Van's telling of the founding of Camelsfoot, about sixty-seven trips over the pass were made in "a reliable Chevy Suburban 4x4 loaded down to the axle" hauling everything from the old world to the promising new world. My family's worldly goods were to take another twenty-seven loads. Improvements had been made by the time we arrived: a large cabin had been built and filled with books and comfortable furniture, followed by an addition with a quiet reading space and two warm bedrooms for Fred and Susan, and Eleanor and Van and their young child, Robin. Others were housed in a small newly built bunkhouse, and six or seven tipis were scattered in the forest around the growing settlement.

The "folks," as the communards referred to themselves, had just begun a massive hydro-electric project. Given our commune's location deep in the mountains we would never be able to plug into the grid, not that any of us would ever have wanted to. In fact, in the valley below us the logging road from town still afforded no grid hook-up or phone service nearer than the St'át'imc community halfway to Lillooet. At certain times of the year it was all the highway engineers could do to keep the road open with its constant sloughing and avalanche problems. The Camelsfoot ambition was to become self-sufficient, with an independent power system that would generate enough electricity for a small village of about fifty individuals. Ambitious, indeed. Kip and I felt that they needed our help, and this project was a big motivator for our taking the plunge, or perhaps more aptly put, the "ascent to Camelsfoot."

A six-foot-deep trench would be dug by backhoe a couple of miles across a long hillside to the water intake. White PVC pipe,

eight inches in diameter, glued together every twelve feet, would then be placed in the bed. Then the plan called for Len, a friend from down in the valley, to come with his chainsaw and his skill and create a giant, insulated log box to house the end of the pipe and all the fancy fittings. The penstock would then be installed much closer to home. The penstock is a smaller pipe that joins the other end of the water-line and drops down a very steep slope, bringing water to the heavy-duty turbine to turn the generator and make electricity. Power from water. Amazing to me. But we were a long way from this miracle.

*Fred and Susan loading Ike with pipe. Two miles of it had to come over the pass this way, bit by bit.*

When my little family arrived Camelsfoot didn't yet have "power from water." We didn't even have running water. In the cookshack we had a forty-five-gallon drum turned on its side and fashioned into a hot water tank, which needed filling every day with five-gallon buckets of water hauled from the creek two at a time over rough terrain. Meeting daily hot water needs for sixteen people was no small task, given the hauling of water and chopping of wood required. The hot water barrel had a separate firebox attached to the same rickety chimney as our beloved cook stove. Even with both of these fires going full blast, the cookshack floor still froze our feet in winter. Cups and glasses left on the table overnight were frozen to the surface in the morning. And, of course, we didn't have any electricity save from the noisy generator that was only used to run the wringer washing machine. Evening light came from hissing white gas lamps, all of which needed daily maintenance. Our single barrel of gasoline was precious, and carefully rationed. Ike hauled it in over the pass as late as possible in the fall before the road had to be closed for many months. It would be April or May before the road would be safe to drive again.

The hydro-electric project was a daunting prospect for this group of intellectuals, who would prefer to be naked in the meadow with their books and instant coffee. Kip and I were intellectuals too, but we were also practical people and could see that we would need all the help we could get to complete this engineering feat while also keeping daily life going. Besides, we wanted a good reason to explain to friends and family, and even ourselves, why we had left our promising young professional lives to join a commune deep in the mountainous southern interior of BC.

Our parents, we felt, wouldn't understand the other reasons, equally valid to us, for such a drastic shift in our life direction. While Willie and Shannon were with their father in Ontario, Julie, Kip and I had spent most of the summer driving around the province looking at towns and cities, considering other scenarios for our family. We were after a home, a real home, not just a nuclear family. We wanted to belong to somewhere, to some place and people. More than this, we felt that we could change the world with the very actions of our lives.

All of this was in my mind as I made my way up the trail. And I was nervous. I knew Shannon was upset with me. We had only just picked up her and Willie from the airport in Vancouver, and

*We moved everything from the Nass to the Yalakom . . . even the chickens.*

I agreed with Shannon that we hadn't consulted them properly before making this huge shift in their lives. We couldn't. Our little house near New Aiyansh in Nisga'a territory north of Terrace, a trapper's shack in days gone by, had sold quickly and new owners were moving in in a matter of weeks. And while I believed in the richness of the experience that was before us and knew it would, at the very least, be interesting to Shannon, I also knew that she loved her father very much and I feared she might want to return to Ontario. I asked her to give it a year. The anxiety was tough for me. Still, I was excited and could hardly wait to arrive at Camelsfoot.

» » »

My children knew our life had never been ordinary. In late 1977 we had made a break for it, leaving behind all kinds of financial opportunities in Fort McMurray so that we could leave northern Alberta and I could return to university in Vancouver. I remember Shannon saying to me as we drove the 350 miles to Edmonton for the last time, on our way to a new life, "Well, Mom, at least it isn't boring living with you." Not an easy task, I reminded myself.

17

In Fort McMurray I had worked as executive director at the native friendship centre, where my job was to re-establish good relations with the government by cleaning up the books after a botched job by my predecessor. The first six months at my desk were lonely. No one talked to me. What was a white woman doing in this job, anyway? Gradually the elderly Cree couple who looked after the building acknowledged me, brought me cups of tea and little gifts.

I started reading magazines like *Akwesasne Notes*, from the Mohawk in upper New York state. My eyes were opened as I learned what was happening to the First Nations people, and especially what was happening to the Cree in their Athabasca Territory, where I found myself. Thus began my radicalization. I ended up working secretly with the American Indian Movement, not really knowing where all the anger at injustice would take any of us.

But I was single with three children and I soon realized, with the help of my children's insistence, that this was no life for us. At the time the ratio of men to women in Fort McMurray was ten to one, and "fun" on a Friday night was drinking yourself to oblivion. I really wanted a better life and I promised them that I would do something about the situation, but I had no answers. So I would go back to school and see if the smart folks at the university had any direction for us.

When I decided to go to Simon Fraser University a friend in Alberta said to me, "If you go to that school you'll become a radical." Not even knowing what department I would choose, I applied to SFU on the basis of my friend's recommendation that this school would be a good fit for my disenchanted and inquiring self. I plotted and schemed every day. I worked hard and counted every single penny. At work I had a file with all my notes and calculations, and I regularly hauled it out and ran the numbers. The day I got both my letter of acceptance and the forms for the student loan was the day that I knew my freedom was at hand.

It turned out to be the best move I ever made. My little family moved into residence on campus, all four of us crammed into a two-bedroom apartment. For the kids it was heaven. They freely roamed the corridors, the pool, the fields and the forests of this modern university with other children from all around the world. Next door they met a family from Chile with their three girls,

and on the other side of us lived a family from Africa. Julie had a thriving babysitting business. I got a part-time job, and gardened in one of the plots on campus so that we could have good food. I joined the food co-op. After the trailer park in Fort McMud, this life was miraculous. I was full of ambition and energy.

*Our settlement as it was when we arrived in the summer of 1982.*

People called me a feminist, but I couldn't really understand why. I was just living my life with the heartiest of intentions. When my eighty-five-year-old grandmother came from Toronto to visit us she told me frankly that I had to learn to sit still or I'd run out of energy. She was with me when I picked up my first grades: straight

A's. There's something so powerful within a person when they're on their game, acting out their own plans. This was most definitely my case. That feeling of power and liberation was akin to what I felt as I approached Camelsfoot.

» » »

As I walked towards the cabin, the six Yalakom yappers (Fred called them "Cuban bear dogs." They looked like a cross between a Jack Russell and a Chihuahua) started their hysterical welcoming barking. No one could ever sneak into this place unannounced. The big wooden door opened and everyone came out to greet me, including Kip, Julie, Shannon, and Willie, who had all just arrived. What a welcome it was! I unloaded my heavy pack and embraced each and every one, which took a while.

My arrival was nicely timed at happy hour, though alcohol was not allowed on the commune. Fred had a problem with alcohol and, like sugar, it was banned. Fine with me, though Kip did like his pint and in our short life together he had actually brewed his own. Never mind, we didn't really need it. "Where are Fred and Susan?" I asked.

Before anyone answered, we all settled into the overstuffed furniture in the cabin, most clutching coffees with goat's milk. Everyone got quiet. Smiling faces shifted to downcast serious countenances. "Just today," someone said, "Fred was diagnosed with esophageal cancer." It didn't look good. Susan was with him now in Vancouver. "They plan to be home in a few days."

What was meant to be a festive and celebratory moment had turned to one of anxiety and distress over Fred's condition. Not to mention the condition of my sweet darling daughter, who was sitting glumly next to her sister on the couch.

Welcome home!

# TWO

# Our Courage Did Not Quail

My mother was used to receiving only letters from me. I hadn't owned a phone for a few years and even when I did have a phone, I couldn't afford expensive long-distance calls. So I wrote letters. I worked a lot of things out in my correspondence with my mother. Still, I knew she, like Kip's parents, wished she could just pick up the phone and talk to me whenever she felt the urge.

But no, our "phone" at the Foot, recently purchased, was a radio-telephone — which must have taken my mother back to the 1940s and her mother's wall-mounted phone that had to be cranked to connect to an operator, who would connect your call. This is, more or less, how our radio-telephone worked, though ours was connected to a car battery instead of a hand crank. It was really a massive party line. Not wanting to be tied to the phone all day, at Camelsfoot we chose to receive incoming calls during "listening hours" from five to six p.m. every day (when we remembered).

While keeping an ear out for the operator saying our call number, whoever was cooking dinner had the entertainment of listening to one or both sides of a conversation. Usually we heard the voices of lonely men in the bush calling their wives and girl-friends back home. If the caller had the foresight to ask the operator for privacy when asking to be connected then the caller's side of the conversation could be muted, but still the receiver's voice was broadcast load and clear, in our case, throughout our cook-shack. We heard it all! I rarely called my Mom this way and Kip never did. His family lived in England and this was just, well, too "far out."

My mother wrote to me almost right away upon hearing the news of our move to Camelsfoot. She said that this life sounded like a holiday, like some sort of permanent vacation. By this she meant that no one had a job. True enough. We lived off of Fred's pension, any unemployment insurance claims we were lucky enough to receive, and various savings and inheritances. Fred's theory was that, with enough people, there would always be a flow of federal dollars. Still, there was an undercurrent of anxiety about money, at least for me. Who would have to "go out" and work? Maybe one of us would have to join those lonely fellows in camps somewhere "out there."

*Fred was one of the last remaining professors from the great purge*

» » »

How did two promising young academics like myself and my new husband get into such a situation? Well, things that can completely alter the course of your life can happen to anyone. So it has been for me more than once in my life. When I left Fort McMurray in 1977 I was looking for a new kind of life, but didn't know where to look or what, exactly, to look for. I knew what I didn't want: another relationship with another guy who would never be able to accept my children. As I approached the university my eyes were open but my vision was framed by my own priorities.

What I wasn't looking for and didn't expect to find was Kip. He had arrived at SFU after seven years of political work mostly with Melanesian islanders, particularly in what was then the New

22

Hebrides, working to liberate their small nations from the claws of French and English colonialism. They were his employers, and in many ways his adopted brothers and sisters. Some of his close friends were sick and dying as a result of poisoning from the diabolic nuclear testing in Moruroa and the Kwajalein islands tests. Like me in northern Alberta, he knew the real people on the other end of the stick, the peoples whose land and traditions were stolen by the colonialists.

Even as a middle-class lad in England Kip had struggled for the rights of boys in his upper-class public school. Kip earned his way into a snooty institution through hard work and scholarships, eventually achieving the high rank of Head Boy on a platform questioning compulsory football, the wearing of shorts in the middle of winter, and swimming year round in a frigid outdoor swimming pool. Kip was distrustful of authority and near to seething with rage by the time we met, but being at heart a gentle person, he rarely showed this dark side of himself.

Kip pursued me relentlessly at Simon Fraser University: in the library, across the quadrangle, and even in the corridors of the Communications Department, where we were both students. Finally he caught the corner of my eye, and try as I might I couldn't get this irritation out — for that's what he was at first. Then, carefully, I began a love affair with this handsome and interesting man.

Both Kip and I registered for Fred's 400-level course on community and society. I knew that Fred was one of the last remaining professors from the great purge of radical intellectuals at SFU from the early Seventies. I also knew that the administration wanted to get rid of him. They suspected his credentials, his PhB, whatever that might be.

Our department was moving rapidly towards policy and mass media studies. I took courses in Marxism and other critical theorists, but most of these other professors were either raving mad, quite literally, or were speaking in such broad political strokes that none of them were addressing my concerns. After all, like Kip I was no longer an inexperienced young adult. I had seen some of the misery and anger in our society, especially from my experience in Fort McMurray. So I welcomed an opportunity to study with Fred, whose work seemed to at least focus on a critique of society and what we might do about it.

There were only a few students registered for Fred's course. Some had drifted in from the geography department; one woman I knew from a labour history course that we were both taking. She was particularly brilliant, a Marxist and a filmmaker. Others I didn't know.

We got to know Fred's teaching assistants, Glen and Kelly, two single guys the same age as Kip and I. They most always attended class with Fred, which was a good thing as they often "translated" whatever Fred was trying to say into straightforward language, helping students like me to make some sense of Fred's lofty lectures. I wasn't the only student who hadn't done all the reading required to keep up with Fred's esoteric thought. Glen and Kelly were serious intellectuals though, they *had* done the reading. I thought they lived in their heads a lot of the time.

Kelly, Glen, Kip and I regularly attended a discussion group on Wednesday evenings at the Clark House, a big old house in Vancouver where Fred, his partner Susan and others lived. Susan provided an element of friendliness that for me offset the intellectual atmosphere of the off-campus philosophical conversations. She often made cake or dessert to go along with endless cups of instant coffee and herb tea. Her hospitality felt normal to me, but the rest of the social life in this place felt intimidating. I had no experience with focused philosophical conversations. I always sat quietly in a corner somewhere.

Fred usually introduced a topic, like "what is community?" or "how do we decide what to do?" Then he would start talking. Fred was a relative of the legendary John Brown, whose "body lies a-mould'ring in the grave." He grew up on a dude ranch in Wyoming and perhaps always wanted to reclaim the life of his youth.

Instead, he sought community life in one way or another, mostly leaving behind one failed experiment after another. Most impressive to me was his sojourn in Fidel Castro's revolutionary Cuba, where Fred was Fidel's first philosopher at the University of Havana.

At first I thought I understood what he was saying. I was often very excited by his thoughts on community, kinship, caring, but inevitably he started to go sideways on me. I thought that Fred suffered from a wandering intellect. But the others seemed to get where he was going, or at least I thought they did. I knew for sure that I got lost.

*My quest had always seemed just a little too extreme*

Nevertheless, Kip and I agreed Fred might be the only professor in our department who was actually saying anything of value. I think I took three courses, in all; they were all much the same. I felt that his were the very topics that had brought me to SFU in the first place. I was and still am very grateful to have taken Fred's classes.

As a single mother with three children I had spent five years of my life working my way, albeit slowly, to the west coast, where friends told me I should go with my burning questions about how we could live a more caring and supportive life. I had a rough draft in my head of certain elements that I wanted in my new world, though I had never really talked seriously with anybody about the details of my quest. It had always seemed just a little too extreme.

As I go over letters between Fred and Kip and me, and the hand-written notes I took from his courses, I remember a particularly dramatic class. From my archives:

> Human society is disorganized, dis-organized. Modern society is very sick. We have lost the capacity to adapt within our natural environment and never have learned how to adapt to one another. Humanity can not adapt, for it is not an organism, and only organisms adapt. We individuals cannot adapt because, in our species, adaptation is a social process. . . . What do people mean when they say "community"?

Fred talked about caring being institutionalized and how this is not community, this is regulated bureaucracy that is replacing real society, real networks of support. Institutionalized so-called community is what stabilizes the chaos that remains when social relations have been undermined. Fred called for abolishing these institutions and returning caring to the home, to each other, to a living functioning culture. Community, he explained, is being defined by individuals who don't know anything about social life.

*Susan was resplendent, like a Mother Earth goddess*

How can they come up with definitions of something so deeply social? But this was just part of the larger problem.

Fred spoke about a genuine re-organization of society and suggested that to be successful this must be done intentionally, in groups. An authentic decentralized social movement. He railed against those who said we already have community, that we have functioning social relations. Look at our schools, our health care systems, our care of the sick and elderly, he remonstrated. It wasn't hard for us to agree that there were serious problems with top-down, mainstream, institutionalized society. We all had our personal stories.

The reconstruction of community shouldn't be taken on by any one person. This, Fred asserted in class that day,

> is the job for a certain kind of intentional group, namely the inquiry group, in mutual communication . . . We underrate the importance and "reality" of discussion generally, when it stems from hang-ups in vital areas and leads to new kinds of group action. We stand at a historical nexus between man and his society which other less developed cultures will reach after us. What we do here and now will of course affect them sharply. It will also provide for them models, good or bad, to guide them when they reach the same nexus. This could be soon . . .

The Marxist labour historian chimed in, trying to make a point about dialectical materialism. "Who are these people, and what about class issues within this definition of 'community?'" she wanted to know. "Who is making these pronouncements? Who is 'in' and who is 'out?'" Fred argued that there was a paradox in our technological society: that we never, as a species, learned to use our knowledge and our power intelligently. And then he went on about how rational, technical society is becoming less and less reliable and how our problems were actually getting worse and worse.

Leaving her questions on the table, he went further and further into his own view of the world, as he often did. She got up and left the room. We never saw her again. They weren't a match. In fact, I think they were missing each other's points completely. Her interests were in class revolution, while Fred's tended towards social evolution.

Fred, as he often did, left us with his definition of social organization:

> When our species learned, through the cumulative adaptations of culture, the requisite arts, and began seriously to modify its world—closer to the heart's desire?—the effect was to place the further direction of our actual evolution in our own hands. The prospects are staggering: Man has become the only animal capable of changing its own nature.

I often felt dumbstruck. I got it, yet I felt disoriented and lacking a grounding in the required reading. Or what was it? Still, even in my confusion, Fred was saying something that spoke directly to my questions and, of all the brainiacs at the university, his was the only voice that came close to addressing my problems.

And there was something very gentle and charming about this fellow. He was not just a scholar. No, I sensed about Fred a man who could do things, who had some knowledge of the real and natural world. I liked that very much. Susan, too, was resplendent, like a Mother Earth goddess. She fed us well on Wednesday nights, and this was far from just a light snack. This was an act of real caring, beyond the esoteric. I got that too.

During our courtship, Kip and I both agreed that the nuclear family is just too thin-on-the-ground, too fragile to support our children and ourselves, and that we wanted a context, something material in which to set that theory into action. So, with the hope of stimulating some serious interest, we took this discussion of community from Fred's classroom and the Clark House meetings to other friends, testing it on them to see if these ideas about community made any sense beyond the lecture hall. Oddly enough, our friends were often argumentative and difficult, always giving many reasons why it couldn't possibly work, why it was folly. No one believed in the possibility of making community as Kip and I did. Were we naive and optimistic? I'll never know for sure.

No doubt there were many factors that led us towards Camelsfoot, but our time at SFU was pivotal. We were both "on track" — coming to the end of our degree programs, building up a reputation with an alternative but intellectual crowd in academia, government, and native and non-native communities, heading towards successful careers of some sort. Yet I knew clearly that society's assumption that one person, namely me, could be responsible for three children all by myself was foolish (naive and optimistic?). I knew this to be ridiculous.

We were also losing patience with most of the offerings in our department. Kip was disenchanted with the university and fed up with political theory; he had no time for centralist solutions, like those offered by Marxists. Both of us were critical of the status quo, looking for an antidote. Then we were introduced to Fred Brown. Our heads turned and we glimpsed a different future. With great courage and a spirit of risk-taking, we stepped off our well-groomed path and followed that new direction. Our lives went one way and not the other.

»    »    »

In the spring of the first year of my master's program I attended a job fair on campus at SFU and applied for, and got, a job with Northwest

Community College in Terrace. I was to be the first adult educator in New Aiyansh, a small Nisga'a village in the Nass River valley. With the help of our professors, Kip and I decided to put our studies on hold just long enough to move up north; we agreed to resume our course work by correspondence over the winter.

We found a renovated trapper's shack just outside of New Aiyansh that had come up for rent. Originally built in the 1940s, the cabin stood in an enchanting cedar and spruce forest on the edge of lava fields on the banks of the Tseax River, a small tributary of the mighty Nass River. This was the perfect place for us to recover from the concrete bunkers of SFU. Its current owners were American draft resisters who were moving back to the US. Over the years these folks had enlarged the original log

*Our heads turned and we glimpsed a different future*

cabin, added a very small makeshift micro-hydro electric system, and restored the gardens. It was plenty big enough for our little family. Kip and I were thrilled. The kids were excited, too.

We spent only two years in Nisga'a territory but this precious time away from the university and the comforts of a city life taught us much about the physical requirements of taking care of ourselves in the bush — knowledge that would serve us well in the years to come in the Yalakom valley. During our time on the Tseax, we lived through a weeklong snowstorm that blanketed the region in many feet of snow. So serious was this storm that several Nisga'a men snowshoed the few miles from the village to our cabin just to make sure we were alright. Wonderfully for us, we could now use our cross-country skis as transportation, or travel by snow machine with its trailing sleigh that hauled the whole family. What a life we had! But it was a borrowed life, in a way. We were in Nisga'a territory and knew in our hearts that we could never truly belong.

Shortly after moving north we learned that Fred and Susan and the others from the Clark House group had already acted on their ambition to create community: this collection of renegade folks was now living in the Yalakom valley, thirty kilometres or so from Lillooet in dry ponderosa pine/Douglas fir country, at the confluence of the Bridge and Yalakom rivers. Fred decided to retire after strong encouragement from the university establishment, who just didn't understand his work at all. Kip and I, though mostly Kip, kept up a vigorous correspondence primarily with Fred, though sometimes Van wrote as well. Amongst the theory and philosophy came the news that Fred and company had their eye on a very special 160-acre piece of property up a mountain valley, completely surrounded by Crown land, known locally as Camelsfoot. Once a wilderness school, this quarter section was the perfect place to set the dream into reality. Soon a deal was made.

*We started to see our own quest as real and achievable*

Other major changes were happening. Eleanor and Van had a baby girl, Robin, who added an element of delight and hopefulness to the social atmosphere. And, quite suddenly and tragically, Eleanor's mother had passed away, leaving Eleanor with a substantial inheritance. With this money, Fred and friends were able to seriously consider developing the infrastructure at their new Shangri-La to include the much-needed hydro-electric system. But the project was huge and complex. After all, Camelsfoot was located deep in a mountain valley, miles away from any real road.

Try as we did to imagine ourselves settling on the banks of the Tseax, Kip and I knew that we would always be outsiders. Far more compelling was the idea we were developing through our correspondence with Fred, of intentionally creating our own viable, caring, living culture, based on our own collective intelligence and inquiry. We learned from Fred that we were not the first to experiment with this sort of idea. The more we learned the historical and literary context of people who inspired each other towards a new and better world, the more we started to see our own quest as real and achievable.

In April Fred wrote to us:

Summer hasn't really struck here yet (although it is now beautifully clear and sunny — still −3° C at night). It has snowed a couple of times, warmed up in a chilly way, and *blown* as it is blowing now. Reminding me that just today, April 12, one hundred and thirty years ago the Brook Farmers gathered in their parlor with Hawthorne by a roaring fire, to dream dreams very similar to ours and watched the wind blow drifts of snow across their newly acquired (April 1) Elysian Fields.

Fred quoted the character Miles Cloverdale, from Nathaniel Hawthorne's novel *The Blithedale Romance*:

But our courage did not quail. We would not allow ourselves to be depressed by the snowdrift trailing past the window, any more than if it had been the sigh of a summer wind among rustling boughs. There have been few brighter seasons for us than that. If ever men might lawfully dream awake, and give utterance to their wildest visions without dread of laughter of scorn on the part of the audience, yes, and speak of earthly happiness, for themselves and mankind, as an object to be hopefully striven for, and probably attained, we who made that little semi-circle round the blazing fire were those very men. We had left the rusty iron framework of society behind us; we had broke through many hindrances that are powerful enough to keep most people on the weary treadmills of the established system, even while they feel its irksomeness almost as intolerable as we did. We had stepped down from the pulpit; we had flung aside the pen; we had shut up the ledger; we had thrown off that sweet, bewitching, enervating indolence, which is better, after all, than most of the enjoyments within moral mortal grasp. It was our purpose — a generous one, certainly, and absurd no doubt, in full proportion with its generosity — to give up whatever we had heretofore attained, for the sake of showing mankind the example of a life governed by other than the false and cruel principles on which human society has all along been based.*

---

\* Nathaniel Hawthorne, *The Blithedale Romance*. Boston, 1852; Project Gutenberg, 2008. Chapter III, para. 17.

Fred went on in his letter to say how difficult it was to stop quoting from this speech, though he added that Nathanial Hawthorne was much better writing about community than actually living his life according to these principles.

In the spring of 1982 we took our family to visit Camelsfoot. Scott and Bonnie Mae were the main designers of the power project, and they went over the details of the plan with us: miles of water line, pipe to be buried six feet deep along the hillside, major and complicated equipment to purchase. If I thought Fred's intellect was opaque to me, this technical stuff was even more so. The communards were so confident, though, that I became convinced they could accomplish the task. Nevertheless, Kip and I thought they could use some help. We were, by now, highly inspired. Real things were definitely happening.

That same spring our little trapper's shack in the Nass Valley went up for sale and was quickly bought. We had known the moment the "for sale" sign went up that our tenancy would likely be limited. Before we knew it we received notice to vacate by the end of August. Having briefly considered buying the cabin ourselves and deciding against it, we now wondered what to do, where to go next. Both of us were serious candidates for jobs in Terrace at the community college, but that lifestyle paled in comparison to the call of the commune.

The Camelsfoot folks invited us to join them. We were not surprised; it had felt like a courtship for some time. We visited Camelsfoot again in late July. This time it was just Julie, Kip, and me; Shannon and Willie were still at their father's place in Ontario for their annual visit. Shortly after this visit Kip wrote a general letter to the commune:

> We were scarcely over the pass in faithful Ike [Camelsfoot's 4x4] when it began to dawn on us that "a decision" had been made during our excellent visit with you, and was just waiting to be discovered! By the time we had reached Lillooet, safely left Ike at the Shell station, and been to the Caravan Stage Company's

show, we were sure that *something* was different . . . It turns out, of course, that we were realizing that we had decided to join you folks at Camelsfoot — as quickly as possible!

So we had a fun journey home over the next two days, speculating on some of the details of moving our lives through Culture Gap, over the mountain . . . We're all three of us *very* excited at the thought, and just bursting to get on with it. After all, there's a whole New World to be built, and we've been procrastinating long enough!

Fred wrote back with enthusiasm from everyone for our decision. By the end of August, Kip and I and Julie had miraculously organized ourselves and all our possessions into categories: some things for the Clark House, and most things for loading into Ike to bring over the pass into Camelsfoot, from my piano to our laying hens to books and toys. We make the long drive from the Nass Valley to the Yalakom River Valley. A life-changing decision, a major shift in direction, had been made and acted upon.

I thought I knew what I was getting into. Of course, I didn't really. Though we do our best to set the scene, no one ever really knows what's going to happen to them. Right from the beginning things were not as we expected.

*Kelly reaches for the frisbee as goats graze in the meadow.*

# THREE

# How Do We Decide
# What to Do?

Every morning we gathered together outside the cabin in rickety adirondack chairs, around an unused, makeshift fire pit, to self-consciously try to organize ourselves, if only for the next twelve hours. Some of us came from families of wealth, some from middle-class backgrounds, some were successful self-made people, some working class. There were Americans, Canadians, Europeans; some with children, some without. All of us showed up, women and men, children and pets. I liked it this way. We were all responsible, all in this together, all wondering what our day would look like. Our second cups of coffee were clutched in our hands. Dogs had found their masters and claimed their rightful laps after a cursory sniff for lost bits of breakfast. On the edges of the circle, the kids were anxiously lurking, wondering if they couldn't just *do* something. They were impatient, as children are, with adults droning on and on. But there was so much to consider.

While I sometimes thought I knew why I was at Camelsfoot, I could only guess what motivated others, and even then that guesswork would probably end up being superficial. All were highly educated and enthusiastically embraced Fred's ideas of creating a culture based on gentler, kinder principals than those of the society we had rejected. Our life together at Camelsfoot was both physically difficult and emotionally confusing, yet all of us were committed to the challenge.

Of course, each of us had our own agenda. I was mostly concerned about what my children would be doing during the day, and who would be cleaning up and preparing meals, chopping wood, these kinds of everyday requirements. Others felt an urgency to do the intellectual work: writing, reading, strategizing on how to get our ideas in print. Still others of us were concerned with our mega-projects: the massive plans for gardens and orchards, and the increasing domination of the hydro-electric project, which sometimes demanded that all hands be put to the task. It was a huge project and would cause anybody to be rattled. It involved a lot of money and many, many details that were completely beyond me. Some of us had health issues that regularly dictated what could and couldn't be done. Some were obsessed with political and economic concerns of the "outside" world, and wanted to engage in the emerging Green parties in Canada and Europe.

I recall endless conversation about the tension between the "Realos" and the "Fundis," between those in the emerging German Green Party who wanted to achieve something within the system and those who wanted to stick to basic principles without compromise. This angst in our own process, for that is what it really was, was made more real to us by the relentless pressure on our immediate environment from the logging and mining companies. Should we, for instance, work with the logging company and the Ministry of Forests, or should we just spike the trees, saving them once and for all? Which camp did we fall into? Realos or Fundis? Similarly in our morning circle at Camelsfoot. We were just sixteen people yet we created a very complex social situation. Do we bend and compromise or do we stick to our ideals? Regardless, we had to make daily decisions, even if just on how to carry out the responsibilities of the day.

Almost from the beginning I sensed tensions in the circle that I did not yet understand: resistance from some, simmering anger and resentment from others, even tears. Fred and Kelly always seemed to be sparring, but I couldn't follow the reasoning on either side.

Kelly had come up the trail with Glen the day before to stay at Camelsfoot for a few days. Glen was a semi-permanent resident at Camelsfoot; he kept a place in Vancouver. His mother still lived there and he was responsible for her in many ways. Kelly also went back and forth between Camelsfoot and Vancouver and had only recently given up his truck driving job. He practiced zen buddhism. This, and other issues less clear to me, put him at odds with Fred.

*I recall endless conversation about the tension between the 'Realos' and the 'Fundis'*

I was glad when both Kelly and Glen were here. They were very helpful around difficult conversations. Each of them had a knack for drawing out from people what they really meant to say, getting beyond innuendos and vague assumptions. Glen was kindly and entertaining. Even the kids loved his stories. Mostly, I think, it was the way he told them, his hands gesticulating and his face all smiles. There often was a good laugh. And Kelly really helped out with the canning. He was maniacal about it, figuring we'd need eighty-five quarts of everything. He would process apples into applesauce until late at night, just to get it done. Okay, mania can be a bit annoying, but it was great that he took on, and finished, such jobs. I really appreciated the work he did. And he was an excellent drummer on the congas and djembe. Our jungle music improved greatly with Kelly's musicianship.

The only trouble with these two was that they never stayed long enough. Something always pulled them away, even though both of them claimed to be committed to what we were all trying to do. I guessed it was tough being single but Alice pulled it off and it was hard for her, too. I couldn't imagine not having someone close to my heart to help me work out what on earth was going on, and what my part might be in the whole confusing configuration.

» » »

As we gathered our collective wits we would hear the racket from Gordon Pike's machine digging away on the water line for the hydro project, up beyond the meadow. Gordon was a rancher with

a backhoe who lived on the other side of town. He arrived before eight in the morning. We knew he was on time when the sound of his four-stroke motorbike woke us up at 7:45. How did he do it? We had no idea. But every morning for over a month he had driven thirty-five miles from his home to start work, and he'd never been late, rain or shine.

By 11:30 we still didn't have a plan for the day. We were trying to decide what to do while faced, as we constantly were, with the larger question: How does one decide what to do? The milking was done and the chickens were fed. We'd had breakfast. So all was not completely a shambles. But Scott and Bonnie Mae, the forepersons for our hydro-electric project, were anxious to get going, concerned to be leaving Gordon so long on his own. And while we philos-

*Gordon and his machine clearing the wilderness for our water line.*

ophized about who we were and how to proceed, we hadn't yet come to terms with the children, the sweeping, the firewood, hauling the many buckets of water, filling the gas lamps for the evening, who would do the huge pile of dishes and cook dinner, and the ever-present anxiety around how we would find the time to nurture our intellectual life.

» » »

It's great to have lofty thoughts, and it's wonderful to be heady and bright, but the truth is that the dirt under the fingernails from the work of everyday life is every bit as important to what's really going on as most of what the mind conjures up in isolation. By this I mean that the hands and the head work well together, in spite of how so-called western civilization strives to separate them. We have inherited this inefficient duality, which only works when backed up with a high degree of privilege. Really, the hands and the head are a team. In fact, the conversations you have while doing dishes, washing clothes, cooking meals, and so on, are where the serious matters of life are worked and reworked, and where gems of inspiration can appear when least expected.

Conversely, it could also be said that without an intellectual life, with our shoulders always to the grindstone, we become slaves, even to ourselves. I quickly noticed, for example, that work on my little pine needle baskets was more beautiful when my mind was slightly removed from the work, as it was when engaged simultaneously with philosophical talk with my friends in the cabin. So I am certain that bringing the mind and the hands together, rather than valuing one over the other, is a noble, if novel, ambition.

Eleanor referred to the talks we had when working together as "good gossip," a phrase I really like. Our arrogant tendency to measure others with patriarchal yardsticks tends to skew our view of other cultural practices, so we only see what we want to see. But look at the history of land-based tribal cultures, especially at the daily lives of women. Most likely they are in a circle, with their hands busy at something useful, small children with them, and they're talking or singing. And what they're saying to each other is important. It's the stuff of life. It's the story of their lives, told and re-told. The children are listening, and so the ways of the people are passed on.

At Camelsfoot, in our attempt to create a culture of place, we didn't have this totally figured out by any means — but what did emerge was fascinating. There was a haziness, for me, around how our daily lives reflected a truly different way of doing things. From the outset, of course, it was *very* different. Sixteen of us were living together, spending all day every day with each other, with no other distractions — no jobs, no radio or television — only ourselves, living an undivided life. We were constructing how our lives would unfold almost moment to moment, and this was something that none of us, with perhaps the exception of Fred, had ever experienced before.

We had many details to consider and much work to be done all the time. But I was sometimes exasperated by the problem of how to hold on to what we all clamoured for, that which was considered to be truly important. This discernment is the heady work of the mind. There was constant anxiety about getting enough "time at our desks." But maybe we didn't have to be all things to all people all of the time? Maybe some of us were thinkers and some of us were tinkerers, and together we made up a coherent whole? Couldn't we find a way to allow this?

» » »

The kids didn't care about any of this. They just wanted to be released from the morning's planning, and they would be soon enough. A typical day for the ten-year-olds, Willie and Alannah, was idyllic.

Alannah was a budding bibliophile. Before Willie arrived, the adults often had trouble getting her off the couch, so engrossed was she in anything that Van, our literary guide, put in her hands. The library held hundreds of feet of books. Alannah was making her way through the novels section.

Willie, on the other hand, was a born adventurer. His current favourite book was Theodora Kroeber's *Ishi In Two Worlds: A Biography of the Last Wild Indian in North America*.* I thought that he liked the pictures more than anything: real bows and arrows, real

---

* Oakland: University of California Press, 2011 (50th Anniversary Edition).

hunting and fishing, and so on. Willie is a lot like me, I told myself. He wants to do things, and has trouble sitting still.

Together, Willie and Alannah were quite a team. They shared the books they read and then, in a beautiful spritely spirit, wanted nothing more than to head into the mountains to spend their entire day "in character," stretching the stories to fit their world. They sometimes herded the kids, the offspring of our milking goats. They frequently took along a billy pail for tea, a bit of birch bark to light a small fire to heat the water, some rye crisp and peanut butter, and with this sustenance they could extend their day as they lived their literature. It was hard not to think they enjoyed the best of our life together. True freedom.

I envied them, but I had too many respon-sibilities to ever consider such play. I had Shannon and Julie to think of and, like some of the other women, felt compelled to dis-cuss dinner before lunch. Milk would have to be processed into soft cheese, beans simmered, and so on. The laundry seemed endless when all the water had to be hauled and heated by fire, and then the generator cranked to run the wringer washing machine that sat out in the wood-lot. There was a very young child among us, and all of her little clothes needed washing almost daily. And now, with Fred and Susan's return from Van-couver, we had a seriously ill person who required devoted care. Work, work, work . . . and we hadn't gotten out of the wood-lot yet! There was also the emotional labour of dealing with the anxiety my daughters were feeling around their education and, perhaps most importantly, their lost social lives.

Kip and I also needed to build some sort of shelter before winter arrived — which was only a couple of months away. Fred and Susan had given us their tipi, which temporarily housed Wil-lie, Kip and me. Fred and Susan had an indoor bedroom in the addition off the cabin. He needed to be warm and cozy with the

*We had a seriously ill person who required devoted care*

41

cookshack close by for quick instant coffee, which he loved. Julie and Shannon had set up a bedroom in one end of the bunk-house. Alice was on the other side. They all had their privacy, but it was far from ideal. I wanted the five of us to be together as a family.

The plan was to build a pole cabin using lodgepole pine for the purlins, fir logs for the uprights, and locally sawn ponderosa planks for the siding, inside and out. All local material. Only the dreaded pink fibreglass insulation, the nails, and the steel roofing would come from town. Kip had never built anything of this size before. I knew one end of a hammer from the other, and was a good helper, but I was no builder. Good thing Kip was inventive and determined enough to take on the challenge of constructing this small dwelling, and with precious little money to work with.

What we hadn't thought of was how difficult it was going to be to work with round logs and square timbers at the same time, and all with hand tools, save the chain saw. The problem of scribing the logs and making everything reasonably tight was Kip's. But somehow I had to find time in my day to peel poles — lots of them.

I told my daughters this was a fine opportunity for hands-on learning, hoping they would pick up the adze and the log peeler and give me a hand. I thought Julie might be interested in the scribing as she had a mathematical mind. Shannon was most definitely interested in seeing the pole cabin built, so she agreed to help peel. It was tough work, though satisfying. Peeling logs works best in the spring when the sap is fresh. It was September, though, and bark can be tricky to get off in nice long strips. Nevertheless we worked together as best we could. I could see that Shannon was giving the whole experience a chance. She was a sweet and tender child and I knew this wasn't easy for her. I was grateful and relieved every time I saw her smile.

» » »

These were just some of the components we grappled with in the late morning sun as we worked hard at making up our day.

Amazingly, we always came up with a plan. It felt great to achieve a sense of order, even if just for the day.

There were many layers of complexity, some lurking below the surface, unacknowledged. It was a complicated life, much more detailed than for most nuclear families, but I loved the way we organized ourselves. We always tried to have at least two folks per job. Making dinner, for example, was much too big an undertaking for one person. There might be twenty people around the table. And the children's education was a big topic. We did our best, of that there can be no doubt. Everyone wanted this experiment to go forward, to work, whatever that meant.

But we weren't tribal people. Things weren't already in place . . . far, far from it. We had to act "as if," Van kept reminding me. As if we had it culturally together when in fact we were a collection of self-imposed exiles from western civilization. And, as we told ourselves over and over again, western civilization is fraught with barriers to an integrated life. As I suspected then, we didn't know the half of it.

And so on and on through another day at Camelsfoot. A bit clumsy getting started but, hey, Rome wasn't built in a day. Rome, did you say?

# FOUR

# Camelsfoot Meets Eaglestarr

I slept in a tipi so it was almost like sleeping outside. The sounds beyond the thin canvas walls were immediate. Every morning I waked to the rooster's announcement to the world that he was here, out and about, and that the hens could now safely come out of the coop. Being a mother, my habit was to get up early, too. I loved the morning light, the feeling of calm before everyone else swooped into the cookshack. We were all "in residence" this early spring morning so there would eventually be quite a crowd. I doubted that the dishes were done from last night. This discouraged me from getting up but I did anyway. First thing to do was light the fire in the cookstove and get the water on to boil for coffee. Many of us required coffee just to begin to be pleasant.

There was a full house last night for dinner, a fabulous meal cooked by Bonnie Mae and Kip: goat curry with pineapple chunks and toasted coconut, heaps of rice, and a huge apple crisp for dessert. It was amazing that all sixteen of us could fit around one long plywood table, but we did. Shoulder to shoulder. To have us all together felt like a celebration. But, with sixteen folks, the dishes were a big job to take on. I hated the mess, though I was learning that it wasn't always my responsibility to clean up. To my delight, when I opened the door the kitchen was clean. I suspected that it was Glen who had cleaned up. He was a night-owl and probably did the dishes after everyone else went to bed. He never cooked, but he often did the dishes.

When someone else cooked, I felt freed up. Usually Van and I would go play our pianos together. And what a treat that was for me! Not only was I not cooking for a change but I got to make music with Van, who I considered an accomplished pianist. And our music made people happy. While it seemed perfectly appropriate to Van and I to each have our own pianos, visitors marvelled at the luxury of it.

When I got up Kelly had already lit the fire and put the porridge on, and there was boiling water in the kettle. He was an early bird, too. I started grinding coffee in the hand grinder mounted on the counter. I decided I had better grind lots this morning. Susan came in and made a cup of tea for herself and a cup of instant coffee for Fred. Not much quiet time this morning. In fact, none, as the kids soon arrived, followed by Eleanor with little Robin slung on her hip. The cacophony began. Willie and Alannah offered to take Robin for a walk in the afternoon. Willie carried her well in "Gerry," the kid-carrier backpack named after its manufacturer. Robin loved being with the older kids. It was wonderful to have a little one there to round out the generations.

After breakfast, we headed to the cabin to plan the day. Susan suggested we spend some time in the tree nursery in the lower garden to do a little pruning and grafting, and maybe have a cup of tea and hang out for awhile in the sunshine. Fred wouldn't come, it was too hard for him, but he would be fine without Susan for a few hours. Most of us decided to go.

Alice stayed behind. She didn't feel well. Again. Her allergies were really dreadful. Not only did she suffer from wheat and dairy sensitivities but we suspected that the moulds that lingered in the old wooden walls and floors, and whatever laid beneath them, were troublesome to her. Some of us thought of Alice like the proverbial canary in a mineshaft, tipping us off to hidden health hazards. This

*Alannah (far left) and*
*Glen (second from*
*right) are welcomed by*
*young Robin, Bonnie*
*Mae, Julie, a Yalakom*
*yapper and Alice.*

was one of those days when Alice would most likely go back to bed. There was nothing much we could do for her.

So, with lunch in hand, about eight of us headed through the forest towards the garden. It took about fifteen minutes to reach the clearing beside the rushing creek. The remains of a settler's cabin from many decades earlier were crumbling next to the hillside. Susan had planted asparagus seedlings inside it, where the floor used to be — a brilliant idea. Just looking at the hundreds of little ferns made me salivate, but they wouldn't be edible for a couple of years.

Susan had started the nursery a few years ago and now there were hundreds of hazelnut and apricot trees. Only a few of these young trees actually produced any fruit, and it wasn't much. Susan was a bit of a fruit tree megalomaniac though, and the sheer quantity of seedlings and rootstocks had been an issue for some time. No one seemed to be able to help her limit her ambitions. For some,

it was a sore point. Nevertheless, the young trees needed care, and Kip was especially excited to learn how to prune and graft. Susan was a great teacher, with years of experience working in gardens with children.

*Judith, Susan, and Julie heeling in new rootstocks.*

» » »

With our hands down in our work, it must have been easy for Eaglestarr to watch us from above the garden, undetected. At some point I did get an uneasy feeling, like I was being watched. I don't recall which one of us first spotted him sitting on the side of the trail. He wore long braids and a beaded jacket. He was the real deal. It was a shock to see someone just appear like that, let alone an Indian man complete with medicine pouch and walking stick. He was just looking at us. When he realized that we knew he was there, he got up and walked towards us.

47

Willie was overjoyed. Here was a real live Indian. Willie had read about Ishi, the sad story of the so-called "last wild Indian" in North America. I knew that my son imagined himself to be transformed eventually, somehow, into a man of the woods, capable with bow and arrow, able to survive in the natural world around him. It was a wonderful aspiration, and we had all encouraged him.

Amazingly enough, Eaglestarr had come to us with a mission: to teach us about the traditional sweat lodge. He explained that this was his purpose in life, given to him by his elders. His assigned task, as he saw it, was to teach us how to build a sweat, how to conduct ourselves in the ceremony, and the meaning of the whole experience.

We were incredulous. Walking that trail was no easy task, and Eaglestarr had a serious limp and some deformity as a result, we would learn, of suffering polio as a young child in his home territory in northern Manitoba.

But we felt that our remote and isolated existence had just been shattered. It's three o'clock in the afternoon, some of us muttered. What about dinner? What about the kids? Fred? The animals? What about our plan for the rest of the day? Is our whole day's work supposed to stop and adjust to this man who commands such authority? Whom we don't even know?

We packed up and, with Eaglestarr in tow, headed back home. Willie and Alannah, being ten years old and thrilled at this unexpected turn of events, were fully awake and present, and stayed close to Eaglestarr, hoping to help. Indeed they did. He sent them into the forest to find twelve thin but long willow trees. Meanwhile, Eaglestarr drew a large circle on the flat near the creek. He instructed others to dig twelve holes equally spaced around the circumference. The willows arrived and he — along with a couple of us under his careful direction, and in his very particular way — bent the saplings and put them into the freshly dug holes. We carefully interweaved the tops of the curved green saplings to form the dome shape of the sweat lodge. Eaglestarr told us that once the willows are in the ground, the sweat is alive and must be treated as one would treat one's mother.

The new sweat lodge's framework needed covering. We opted for some of the old carpets that we had hauled over the pass to use as floor coverings for the dirt floors of tipis. Next came the fire that would heat the twenty medium-sized rocks that still needed to be found. We needed a lot of firewood because this was going to last for hours.

We were all involved by now. Even Fred was hanging around the edges. He was no stranger to sweat lodges, having lived in Tahltan country way up in the Stikine River territory for several years. Fred became as close to that community as was possible for a white man at that time.

*Being in the sweat was like being in the belly of the earth*

We lined the new sweat with fresh cedar boughs and it was finally ready. The fire blazed, the rocks were glowing red. By now it was dark outside, way past dinner time, but no one seemed to care. Kelly lifted the rocks from the fire with a shovel and carefully placed about six of them in the centre of the sweat, doing exactly as he was told.

A drum was fetched from the cabin to accompany Eaglestarr's high-pitched voice. His chanting filled the atmosphere, reaching into the night sky through the tall trees all around us. Some of us tried to join in but the high falsetto needed for Indian singing didn't come easily to our throats.

Being in the sweat was like being in the belly of the earth. Dark, wet, and very hot. Fourteen of us managed to find a place up against each other in the sweet-smelling darkness. There was silence for a long time. Eaglestarr splashed water on the rocks with a fir bough. As it hissed, the steam intensified the heat to almost unbearable proportions.

"We give thanks to grandfather rocks," our new friend and

teacher told us. Hotter and hotter it got as he led us in a traditional prayer, ending with "The energy from the rocks, wood, and water is to heal our bodies and our minds. If the rock cracks, it is to show us that anything can change. All Our Relations."

After a splash in the cold creek, we repeated the cycle again, and again, and again. By late in the evening, we had accomplished the required four rounds. Glen said, on behalf of us all, "Thank you, Eaglestarr, for reminding us not to take each other for granted."

We were exhausted and hungry but all of us saw it through to the end, even the kids, except for little Robin who had long since been put to bed. Back at the cabin we heated up leftover curry and had a fine meal. As the food brought us back to ourselves, we realized that we were all grateful to Eaglestarr, and the sweat. At Camelsfoot, you never knew what was going to happen in a day. Anything can happen to anyone at any time that changes every-thing . . . I was so glad that we all shared this amazing experience. Our life was so rich and full . . . of surprises, and blessings.

» » »

Our relationship with Eaglestarr continued over the years. We never really knew much about his backstory. He wasn't a local person but an intinerant and a loner, an unusual situation for an Indigenous person. In many ways, we took him under our wing, giving him food and shelter and sometimes money when he needed it. From time-to-time we'd get a call on the radiophone, often from Vancou-ver, or he would just show up unannounced, like he did the first time. In the mid–'80s while driving through Michigan on our way to a bioregional congress, Kip and I spotted him hitchhiking. He was on the opposite side of a very busy highway so we couldn't stop, we just kept going and wondered where he was headed. One day someone in the valley received the news that Eaglestarr had died, in Manitoba. He must have gone home when he knew his end was in sight, but who really knows? This is the story we told ourselves.

# FIVE

# Big Food, Big Issues

In late September, Alice approached me with a huge file under her arm. "We need to talk food," she said. "The co-op order has to go in in a few days. What is your family used to eating?"

The co-op Alice referred to was Fed Up. Kip and I had been members of this food co-op centered in Vancouver since our time at SFU. Members from around the province and as far away as the Yukon took turns doing work weeks in the Vancouver warehouse. When we lived near New Aiyansh we were members of the Terrace collective, and so I did a couple of work weeks in the warehouse. It was lots of fun, though serious work. We received shipments, unpacked and shelved the food, then weighed out and repacked large orders for pick up. There was also office work, mostly taking endless inventory and order entries on large sheets of paper and entering member info on file cards.

Fed Up began in 1972, in response to people's needs for high-quality bulk food, especially (but not entirely) in rural areas. Initially Fed Up was funded by a $20,000 grant from the NDP government, but when we were at Camelsfoot it was a vibrant part of BC's alternative community. Fed Up was a real connective force among back-to-the-landers, as well as neighbourhood-centered city dwellers.

Twice a year Fed Up put out a broadsheet called *The Catalyst*. The center spread listed the prices of the goods and commodities available, and the other eight pages wrapped around it were dedicated to the news and views of a member group. Each group took a turn creating these pages, sharing their stories, artwork, and reviews, all of which added a flavour of their different regions.

At Camelsfoot, Alice told me, we ordered with the folks in the valley; our member group was called the Bridge River People. Alice said our turn to create the member pages would most likely be in late winter. I looked forward to getting together and spending a few days hand-crafting them, and I knew Kip would be thrilled at the chance to use his journalist's skills.

*The food systems on the commune were like a dream come true for me*

"So, any favourites? Must haves?"

We pulled out the price list. I couldn't help but notice the wrap-around pages. They looked fascinating to me, but then I'm easily distracted. Headlines like "Arms are for Hugging," "The Art of Seagulling," "The Politics of Coffee." There was even a posting for help in the warehouse for the fair salary of $1,140 a month plus benefits. That's about what I had made the previous year as an adult ed teacher in New Aiyansh.

I could see that Alice just might be losing patience. We started with cheese. "Well, we make a lot of our own," Alice reminded me. "But we do need hard cheese. We like —"

"— we like gouda and cheddar, with a good supply of parmesan to stretch out a spaghetti sauce," I finished enthusiastically.

"Exactly like us. None of the blues, but maybe a little mozzarella."

On it went for a couple of hours. We hit every item and, with very few exceptions, found that my family's diet was more or less the same as the Camelsfoot diet. Sardines and mackerel would be new for us, and Marmite new for others.

Alice totalled the whole thing up when we were finished. I

couldn't believe how much money we were spending — thousands of dollars. "But remember," Alice said, "there are sixteen of us, and this is it. The pass will be closed from the end of October until the end of April. No grocery stores or health food stores within easy access. Nothing is even close to convenient. Anything else we want we'll have to haul on our backs up the trail. I think our order isn't too bad at all. I was expecting more. It's great we have the same tastes; that saves on a lot of extras."

I noted the many rounds of cheese and cases of olive and safflower oils, and a few of the other pricey items like engevita yeast — we'd ordered a forty-five gallon drum of the stuff — on our order form. Every day each of us on the commune knocked back at least one glass of water stirred vigorously with a couple of table-spoons of engevita and a teaspoon of vitamin C crystals. We were all addicted to it. Susan claimed it kept us healthy. Even my kids lined up for it. We also sprinkled the yeast on much of what we ate. Yeast on alfalfa and sunflower seed sprouts doused with olive oil and a dash of cider vinegar was hard to beat!

I was instantly drawn to the food systems on the commune, which were like a dream come true for me. I loved to see huge pots simmering on the stove, and big food projects in general. Cooking for my family of five had always been a pleasure for me. From the time they were in high chairs, preparing food was a time for me and my kids to hang out together. Shannon was usually with me when I was on dinner detail on the cookshack; it was social time for us. She didn't always help out but would if asked. Shannon had a real knack for food presentation. Her dishes could look like works of art.

We didn't have electricity so perishables were stored in securely lidded wooden boxes in the icy cold creek, which worked extremely well. Everything was cooked on or in a cook stove, a versatile piece of equipment that I grew to love. Once the cook learned how to feed the stove in just the right way, every part of the stove's surface could be kept at a different temperature. Several of us baked bread, and once in a while I made a sourdough starter, much to Fred's delight. Bread baked in a wood stove is as good as it gets, though it had to be carefully turned several times to avoid burning on the firebox side of the oven. Not only did the stove cook our food, it heated our kitchen. Our stove had a warming oven above the surface, which was great for culturing yogurt, and a perfect environment for drying empty eggshells, which would then be fed to the hens for some calcium in their diet.

We always had more than enough to eat, but because there were so many of us we were rarely able to eat whatever we wanted. The really tasty things, like hard cheese, eggs, and meat, were rationed. I don't recall ever sitting down to two pork chops, for example, as I might have desired. We never had bacon and eggs for breakfast. That would have meant at least three dozen eggs and several pounds of bacon. Our first meal of the day was most often a massive bowl of porridge, pancakes (Vancakes are still infamous), sometimes with canned or dried fruit, homemade yogurt, and maybe a dollup of fresh cheese. We had buckets, indeed sometimes barrels, of rice and beans, and plenty of oats and flour and grains. Peanut butter and rye tack was a favourite midnight snack. All food, of course, was stored securely in lidded containers otherwise the mice and packrats would have robbed us blind.

We always had a fresh supply of milk. There were six milking goats and a growing herd of kids, a billy goat named Erasmus, and a wether, ironically called Samson, who kept the billy company to give the does a break. All of the kids were weaned, though I suspect they helped themselves now and again when the whole herd was grazing in the mountains. The nannies could brush the kids off with a quick flick of their horns.

Two people milked together twice a day and got three gallons of milk with each session. It took about half an hour, and was a lovely way to visit with a friend. Milking was a peaceful time. It had to be. If you were upset, the goats knew it and wouldn't let their milk down.

As soon as the milk was brought to the cookshack from the barnyard it was strained into gallon jars. The morning milk was run through a separator. This was Willie and Alannah's job, our ten-year-old budding dairy experts. They loved it. They built themselves a step-stool out of bits of lumber so that they could reach the crank. It was funky, but safe enough, and worked well. They took turns turning the crank. With each revolution, the inner workings clanked almost musically. When the children finished the job, they took the contraption apart and washed it with great care, as Susan had taught them.

Their efforts produced skim milk, which some of us preferred over the rich, whole-fat milk, and extremely thick cream, so heavy that spoons literally stood up in it. This was mostly used for quiches, eaten with apple crisp or stewed fruit, or made into cream cheese then mixed with herbs.

Most of the evening milking was made into soft cheese, inoculated with buttermilk or rennet. Chevre was surprisingly simple to

*Eleanor, Van, and Alice keep an eye on Samson, the wether.*

55

make. We would set the spiked milk in stainless steel pots on the back of the warm cook stove in the evening, and by the morning it had heated and cooled. Then we ran a knife through the milk, which by then looked almost like custard, and cut it into squares. Cheesecloth draped over a colander sat ready on the rim of a large pot. We gently poured the curds through the cheesecloth. The birth of curds and whey! Then we would gather the cheesecloth around the curds, squeeze it very gently only once, tie it together at the top, and hang it over the pot to drain, suspended by a long cord attached the ceiling. After a few hours we'd take it down and unwrap it to reveal soft, beautiful, fresh cheese. A gallon of milk netted a pound of fresh cheese. Next we added fresh herbs. Susan grew delicious garlic chives and basil in the greenhouse, and rosemary grew against the cookshack. Sometimes we added a little roasted garlic, but it was precious. Even plain, this fresh cheese was outstanding.

*The seething anger had to be about more than cows and goats*

That was Freedom Cheese, to me. Most of what the goats ate came from the hillsides around us. Okay, there was a little grain at milking times to keep them distracted, but this product was as close to freedom (for the goats and us) as cheese ever gets.

What to do with the endless supply of whey? This was a big problem for me, as I hated to waste anything. Eleanor used it some-times in bread. It worked but bread only uses up a few cups at a time. Bonnie Mae had made soups using whey as stock, but not everyone cared for the taste, myself included. I had read some-where that women (of course) had used it as a floor cleaner. I tried that on the wooden cookshack floor. It worked but the whole place smelled like the wrong end of a dairy for days. That wasn't a popu-lar experiment. We solved the whey problem when we figured out that we could feed it to our three not-so-little pigs. Whey is highly nutritious and the pigs lapped it up with their mash. I was relieved, as we couldn't just throw the whey away. Turning it into bacon and pork chops was a great idea.

Some of us truly loved the goats. Goat's milk, we were told, was very good for us, far superior to cow's milk. And goats are thrifty and smart. Still, not everyone loved the goats; some wanted a cow instead. The goat/cow topic was loaded with acrimony and tension. The commune was so deeply divided on the issue that some folks couldn't stand the goats — didn't like the smell of them, didn't like the milk, and refused to drink it.

Goat intelligence is part of the problem, they said. Goats hate being corralled, for example. And that billy goat was downright mean. At breeding time he was a maniac, peeing all over his beard, his wild eyes looking for a fight with any male, human included, that ventured near him. He attacked Kip one day in the barnyard, and it was frightening. A couple of the other men saw what was going on and were able to restrain Erasmus enough to get him back into his lonely pen. A good fight is foreplay for goats but best done with another goat, not tender peace-loving humans!

Cows, we were told, can be artificially inseminated, eliminating the need to keep dangerous male animals around. Almost every day this toxic debate went on and on. I didn't understand what was at the bottom of the issue. The seething anger that surfaced had to be about more than cows and goats. The exchanges were too heated and emotional to be simply about livestock, but I couldn't put my finger on it. Just another of those things that were here before Kip and I arrived and that I had yet to figure out. For the time being, I was just happy to have fresh milk. I would have loved to try making hard cheese and for that I would prefer cow's milk, but I kept this to myself. Since there was far from consensus on the goat/cow issue, nothing changed, and resentment simmered.

» » »

Bacon and pork chop time came soon enough that second fall after our arrival a year prior. We had raised three pigs over the summer months and slaughtering time nicely coincided with the cooler weather. From the sound of it, one would think I'm an old hand at this. Not at all. I had grown fond of the pigs. Scott warned me to be careful around their pen. "Never fall into the trough," he said. Like I would. "If they get the better of you, they'll eat you. They'll eat anything!" But I still fed them and looked them in the eye from time to time. So did the children.

After much research in Susan's amazing animal husbandry library, we had come up with a plan to slaughter one day and butcher the next. It was going to be a busy and traumatic few days. First we spent a day setting up the site. We set up a huge cauldron made of an old barrel cradled over a fire to heat water for the scalding. We rigged a pulley system to hoist the carcass up high so that it could bleed out and then be lowered into the barrel. Eleanor sharpened the knife she would use to slit the jugular vein immediately after the animal was shot. Van cleaned the gun.

When it was finally time to take their lives I was a total wreck. My daughter Julie, on the other hand, could hardly wait for the butchering. She was a serious biology student. Susan shared Julie's interest and the pair of them were looking forward to the hands-on anatomy lesson. Still, at killing time she decided to hide out in the cookshack with her sister and brother . . . and me. No one seemed to mind.

*Bang!* We heard the shot and knew the pig was dead. Quickly we headed outside and there was Eleanor doing her job. Blood was everywhere. The cauldron was steaming. The men hoisted the dead animal up, sliced off the head and put it in one of the three white plastic five-gallon buckets at the ready. While the carcass was bleeding out, Julie tested the hot water. The gauge was three dips of her finger. If by the third dip she couldn't take the heat, the water was ready. Very quickly the meat — for that's what it had become — was yarded over the forty-five gallon drum and, with strong men on the end of the ropes, dipped into the very hot water. The butchers determined it had spent enough time in the bath to release the coarse bristles for scraping. Up it went again, and someone with a large knife began to cut the carcass in half,

making two sides of pork. One by one as this process was repeated, each was laid out on the table, and the butchers scraped off the hair with scraping knives to leave a clean, smooth skin. By the end of the day we had three heads in buckets and six sides hanging in the root cellar to chill.

*Bonnie Mae, Alice, Julie, and Eleanor scald the pig while I barely look on.*

The next day we butchered the pigs. We used the chart from the *Joy of Cooking* as our guide, and carving a side of pork into chops, ribs, roasts, and so on was surprisingly easy. I was very impressed at the way the cuts turned out.

The butchers handed us trimmings and scraps, and soon they were frying on the cookstove. That night we would eat liver for dinner. The livers were still very fresh and we knew that this was what we were supposed to do. Hunters always eat the liver first. Fortunately, I love this organ meat, but my children and some of the others couldn't stand it, so we made sure there were enough pork bits to go around. The meat was precious and very good. I was extremely excited about the sides of bacon to come, the large roasts for hams, and even the hocks.

We didn't eat all three livers at one meal. They were huge. The rest would have to be frozen with the hearts, which were also huge, and the kidneys. We chilled them overnight secured in the cooler in the creek with our packages of pork chops, ribs, and roasts, so that tomorrow we could take it all to our big freezer plugged in outside Billy Michell's place, located on the reserve halfway to town.

Camelsfoot was lucky he let us do this in exchange for helping with his hydro bill. Without those freezers we would not have been able to raise pigs. We knew Billy, and some of his family, and often saw them in town. Our neighbours were few and far between and it was in everybody's interest to lend a helping hand. Our relationship with Billy Michell seemed healthy to everyone and just the way you'd hope things would work, unlike our relationship with Eaglestarr, who taught us much but in the end needed us more than we needed him. We were always looking for ways to add meaning to our everyday relations with our St'át'imc neighbours. Eleanor would eventually even try to learn their language. Their kindness towards us, as well as their elegant cultural ways, would be revealed to us over and over again as the years went by and our lives became ever more overlapping.

*I had made jellied moose tongue before but I had never faced a head*

Before the butchering, Kip and a few of the other guys had reclaimed the old one-seater outhouse from the scrap pile of lumber waiting for nail-pulling, and set up the phone-booth-like structure in the barnyard. We scrubbed it clean and removed the seat. While Gordon Pike had been here with his machine, he had dug us a magnificent new hole for a brand new three-seater outhouse that was quickly constructed and put to use. We transformed the old outhouse into a smoker, complete with hooks to hang up the precious meat. Outside of it we stacked a good pile of mountain maple to keep the smouldering coals in the tiny stove going day and night for about five days.

It wasn't long before we decided that something had to be done with those heads. I remembered my uncle showing me how to make head cheese once. It was very tasty, and we could use something different to eat for lunch. My uncle had used meat from the grocery store. We had the real thing. Bonnie Mae and I looked it up in *Stocking Up*, and sure enough there was a how-to section on head cheese, also known as souse. While I had made jellied moose tongue before — another fabulous prepared meat — I had never faced a head.

We tooled ourselves up with sharp knives and brushes of all sizes, from tooth brushes to scrubbing brushes. Some parts of the head you just remove and dispose of, but there's a lot of good meat easily accessible. Once cleaned, we simmered it with bay leaves, onions, and peppercorns on the back of the stove for several hours. We did one the first day to see how it all turned out. Once it was done, we were surprised at the amount of meat we harvested from the pot. We removed all the skin, chopped and shredded the meat, and added salt and pepper and lots of finely chopped fresh parley and garlic. We used just enough of the broth to cover the cooked meat, and then put the thick mixture into loaf pans and set them to chill in the creek cooler. When morning arrived, we turned it out of the pans. It looked beautiful: jellied nicely from all the gelatin in the bones, and chock full of meat. And it was very, very good. Everyone liked it!

We had a great idea for some of our product from the next two heads. Although the head cheese would keep for a long time in the cooler, we hoped to trade some of it with Pat and Allison, our rancher neighbours in the valley below us. Their place at the far end the valley — 140 acres of utterly pristine beauty — was really a horse and cow affair. We knew their beef was as good as our pork, and wanted some. Pat, old cowhand that she was, scoffed at the idea of trading our newly minted pork product for her exquisite beef. But then she tasted our head cheese, and like many of the communards, was pleasantly surprised. She agreed that she could use a break from endless beef. Soon we had a deal. I was pretty proud of us for tackling this unusual big food project, and the deal for beef was, well, icing on the cake.

» » »

Though not always anticipated, head cheese wasn't the only unusual meat we ate at Camelsfoot. One day Scott had a brilliant idea, and we had a few extra dollars around thanks to Eleanor's inheritance. For a hundred dollars, he bought ten homing pigeons. They were housed in a giant bird cage constructed over the old outhouse site. We could visit the birds on our way to and from the new outhouse. It seemed perfect, really. They were delightful, cooing lots of the time, adding an element of serenity to the barnyard. In spite of some serious resistance at the outset, we all grew quite fond of these little birds of peace.

Scott started learning how homing pigeons do their job. The plan was for them to take messages, tied to their tiny feet, over the pass to our neighbour's place. He, in turn, would attach his answers to the birds and send them home. How this actually would work, I wasn't sure. But it sounded great.

One morning, however, we woke up to find that each and every one of these beautiful birds had been beheaded. They all lay dead at the bottom of the cage. Every one of us was upset.

The post-mortem didn't take long. "It was a weasel," Fred was certain. "This is what they do. Kill the prey and then come back and take their victims, one at a time. The cage needs to be very, very tight to keep the little creatures out. A weasel can get into almost anything."

Bonnie Mae, even more of a spendthrift than myself, quietly scooped up the bodies and began plucking. She was trained in French cookery in San Francisco and was, without doubt, the most creative cook on the commune. For dinner that night we had a rare treat, indeed: pigeon pie, a $100 pigeon pie! At least their lives, and our investment, had not been all for nothing.

This was the same creative cookery mind that served up organ burgers one night. Who could imagine such a meal but Bonnie Mae? She put all the extra bits from the pigs that no one wanted to eat on their own into the big hand-operated meat grinder, along with onions, garlic and herbs. Fried up with bacon fat, the burgers were a huge hit. Even the non-liver lovers lapped them up.

I learned much from Bonnie Mae's resourcefulness. She had grown up on a farm in northern Alberta and had, I suspected, known hard times. I wondered if this wasn't the cause of her tenacity, which, for better or worse, showed up in other areas of our life together.

»   »   »

Almost everyone contributed in a major way to keeping everyone fed, which required a big effort. Some of us were very familiar with the work needed to keep food on the table, others were new to this challenge but took it on nevertheless, and a few just didn't do much with food at all, except eat it! For me, with three kids, it was second nature and I loved the bigness of it at Camelsfoot. Canning, for example, was easy to get in on, since there's so much preparation and processing involved in making eighty-five quarts of everything: applesauce, pears, cherries, peaches, apricots, tomatoes, plums. Maintaining our diet was a massive undertaking. And there was no trade-off between quality and quantity — we wanted both!

*Willie holds a bobcat that got too close to our chickens.*

I feared becoming oppressed by my favourite occupation, however. I didn't want to be seen as "the cook" because I made really good dinners and loved to share food with friends, or as "the dishwasher" just because I couldn't face a huge pile of dirty dishes as I attempted to prepare a meal. Why did some folks only cook some meals, never venturing beyond the one thing they knew how to prepare? Or others prepared the sloppiest, worst possible meal? For example, whole wheat noodles cooked to such an extent that they had to be carved out of the pot. Or yet another pot of beans and rice. Didn't others understand that food is love?

I felt a bit of an issue creeping under my skin. Maybe my standards were too high? Maybe I was shooting myself in the foot with my own expectations, giving myself too much work when it was my turn to cook dinner and then expecting the next guy to do the same? I feared that if I didn't insist on tasty meals we would get comfortable with the lowest common denominator. Bathtub cleaning was a prime example, embedded as it seemed to be with the attitude of "why should I leave it clean when this is not the way I found it?" Or, and I dreaded this because it would be impossible to address, was there even an attitude of "I can't be asked . . ." that implied privilege? I didn't know. But I did know that I didn't want to work all the time, either. I was not feeling good about it at all.

I couldn't help but wonder if there weren't contradictions emerging between our theory of what was valued and what was not, and our practice at Camelsfoot. If ours was a culture built on the relationships of everyday care and love for each other, then why were food preparation and cleaning still regarded as less important than writing, building, and planning? Were we not just re-creating the same old, same old? I wasn't sure. I didn't know even in myself.

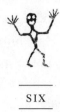

# SIX

# The First Winter

Fred got sicker and sicker as the weeks and months wore on and by winter he often spent the whole day in bed. Susan was an amazing caregiver. I learned a lot from her about how to be with an ill person, knowledge that would stand me in good stead later in my life. She read to him, or sat quietly by his side; rubbed his feet and hands throughout the day to keep the circulation going; fed him densely nutritious food like "essence of beef," which she made almost daily for him, and which he often rejected.

Fred's social life was limited by the amount of energy he had, which Susan knew intimately. Sometimes when one of us hoped for a little time with Fred, we had to leave the room in disappointment. He just couldn't rise to it, and that was difficult to accept for those used to his company and conversation. Van sat with him a lot, trying to get Fred's philosophy on paper before it was too late. Amazingly, Fred took up learning ancient Greek over the winter so that he could read the old texts. Scholarly right until the end.

Willie was in every day. I think sometimes that the boy's energy spilled over into Fred. Out came the ropes, their hands gesticulating this way and that with meaning only the two of them shared. My son learned all kinds of mountaineering tricks at Fred's sick bed: rappelling, rope tying, rifle cleaning, and outrageous acts like balancing on a mountain ledge while leaning into the wind. I braced myself for these antics while at the same time loving that Willie was exposed to such a rare character. Fred was the grandfather Willie never had, and Willie was the sort of grandson that Fred most likely always wanted for himself.

Susan, of course, was a constant presence in the room. Eleanor said quietly to me one day, as we watched Susan go from the cookshack to the addition with yet another cup of instant coffee in hand, that Susan could *really* look after him because we were here taking care of her and everything else. It was true. The rest of us completely supported her dedication to Fred, and took over the rest of the tasks on the commune. Susan didn't have to do any of the daily chores like meal preparation, milking, dishes, firewood, hauling water and so on. I saw this as just the way it should be. She did what she wanted, and her first priority was Fred. Sometimes she was able to turn her attention to the children's education, and that was welcomed, especially by me. But it was in her role as caregiver where I had the greatest respect for her. She was a model for me.

» » »

We took turns leaving the ranch, usually in pairs. While it was fun to get away, it involved strenuous effort. The mountain pass that we drove in summer and fall was impassable in the winter, so any trips to the valley or to town had to be made on foot down the treacherous trail. This meant crampons or ice creepers over our felt pac snow boots, and heavy back packs to haul mail and parcels and exotic treats from the grocery store. Carrying home everyone's mail and treats from town really added a load to the slow walk back up the trail. In spite of this, a trip to town could be a welcome relief. Sometimes you could even shower at the local laundromat — and we'd be sure to stop for lunch at the Reynolds hotel in Lillooet, usually a clubhouse sandwich and fries.

Early in the winter, Shannon and I headed for town. We could hardly wait for lunch. We talked about bacon and those clubhouse sandwiches all the way down the trail. After lunch and picking up the mail we stopped briefly at the Country Store, a little grocery store on the edge of town. We couldn't resist the tropical fruit and thought everyone would enjoy some. Oranges and grapefruits for sixteen or more people made a load and a half! Our packs were much too heavy. I could hardly lift mine up. Shannon was stalwart — a tough kid in more ways than one. We made it, but we wouldn't do it again. It was just not worth the effort.

One of several tipis at *Camelsfoot*.

»   »   »

By late fall, Julie had her own tipi and we moved Shannon into the tipi with Kip and I and Willie. Sometimes the temperature dipped to minus twenty. Even in the bunk-house, now used by Bonnie Mae, Scott and Alannah on one side, and Alice on the other, the little stoves didn't hold a fire all night long, and the inside temperature quickly fell to that of the outside. To prepare for the cold I made big wool bat duvets for two of my children; the rest of our family had down sleeping bags and extra wool blankets. The tipis were heated with a fire in the centre pit that was started at seven o'clock and fed continuously until we went to bed around ten. When we lit the fire we hung bedding on ropes around the circumference to warm up the blankets and flannelette sheets. The ropes were there to string up the o'zan, a five-foot rain flap that helped keep the fire's warmth in and reduced drafts.

With the bedding off the beds, the mattresses were exposed to the warmth of the fire. Everything helped. We had a few rocks — actually soapstone plates we'd liberated from the bottom of old crock pots — that we heated up during the evening on the big wood stove in the cabin. At bedtime we wrapped the rocks in towels and, by the light of "bugs," stout tin cans slung with a wire handle and a candle thrust through the long side, we headed to the tipi. It was only a hundred yards or so down the alleyway from the cabin. Once inside, we quickly put our beds together and, with most of our clothes off save our toques and socks, and sometimes wearing long johns and flannelette pajamas, we got into our beds with our hot rocks and fell asleep while watching the fire dwindle.

*Down "the alleyway"*
*in wintertime.*

When I waked in the night there was always the beauty of the night sky and the stars to gaze at through the smoke hole overhead. The stars were brilliant in the crisp air, and it was easy to drift back to sleep in their presence. There were no other sounds except the odd wild creature, one of the wilderness gods that we lived with, most likely a coyote or an owl. Sometimes, when it was snowing out, being inside a tipi felt like a spiritual experience, perhaps akin to being in the womb. The quiet was like nothing I'd experienced, deep, dark and utterly peaceful.

Except for one night. It started to snow around eight at night, and was building up to quite a good dump as we went to bed. We tucked into our warm bedding and soon fell asleep. Before long, there was a scream from Shannon. We were all awake in an instant. The child was covered in snow! Being novice tipi dwellers, it never occurred to us that we would need to pay attention to the snow load around the smoke flaps, especially once the fire died down. What a misery! Luckily, it was dry snow and easily brushed away. Kip lit the fire again, and we all settled down. I told myself that Shannon would enjoy telling her own children this story one day.

» » »

With the endless complications we seemed to have to accommodate on the commune, work on the water-line for the massive (to us) hydro-electric project proceeded at a snail's pace. Anxiety and frustration surrounded it like heavy fog. We wanted nothing more than clean air to breathe at night, instead of the off-gassing from the gas lamps, and we yearned for running water and hot baths. Still, the work on the project dragged on through the fall and stopped dead as winter descended. The water-line did not get buried in time for winter power and water. That meant we had to haul water and live with hissing gas lamps at night all through the dark of winter.

We didn't get the pole cabin finished before winter either. Most days allowed for Kip and I to continue with a little work on it, but there were so many pressing projects and so many issues around each of them. Often we had to interrupt work on our cabin to work on the water line, or help with thirty cases of apples, or unpack the huge food co-op order, or, or, or . . . None of us could put our own project first and foremost every day, which everyone found difficult to accept sometimes. This consternation extended those morning gatherings in the cabin or the adirondack chairs, almost grid-locking our already fragile decision-making.

While other projects languished, our disappointment was tempered by the added interest of our newly arrived horses. In early

November, while our mountain road was still open for another few weeks, Fred and Susan left for a trip up north to buy horses. In spite of Fred's weakened condition, we felt he would make the best decisions around what horses would work for our needs. They bought two. This meant we would have to make many trips over the pass with Ike loaded inside and out, hauling enough hay to feed the horses over the winter. Like we needed more projects! But the horses were part of the grand plan.

There was grumbling about this decision; I knew it was not embraced by everyone. I felt happy not to have been involved in all the details of the master plan. Kip and I had joined this scene that already had ongoing ambitions so we accepted the plan and didn't feel offended, but others did. Horses, it was felt by some, were necessary elements for a coherent and integrated life in our particular landscape. We were not the only folks in the area to have horses. Besides Pat and Allison, who had many on their ranch, others in the valley kept a horse or two as work animals and for transportation. The right horse would be able to navigate narrow mountain trails, and could be packed using the difficult diamond hitch that some of us, especially Willie, were diligently practicing. Besides, as Scotty loved to say mostly for the shock value, "unlike a tractor, at least when a horse is finished you can eat 'em."

I secretly longed for lots of opportunities to ride. Fred grew up with horses in the Grand Tetons on a dude ranch owned by his family, and he rode like a cowboy. Van went to a classy military school in the United States, and he rode like an aristocrat. Both were highly skilled in their different ways. The rest of us were a little in awe. Kip, being a middle class Englishman, really wasn't interested. Horses, to him, were part of the ruling class, ridden during the fox hunt or around the village by snooty women donning fancy boots and riding gear. He just didn't get it, and hadn't been in the "wild" west long enough to understand that horses could be an integral part of a working ranch. Willie, of course, saw himself as a budding cowboy under Fred's guidance and training.

Our two new horses were percheron/morgan crosses, huge animals. We did nothing with them all winter long but feed them and move them from their stalls in the barn to the meadow and back again. I wanted to be a part of their care and I really wanted to ride, but I was shy because I lacked knowledge, and perhaps a little courage.

One day I got my chance to ride. Fred was dressed and outside (with his cane, of course), giving instructions to Van about this and that to do with the chainsaw. Julie had ridden Dan, one of our neighbour's horses, up the trail — a dangerous ride in my opinion, but she had made it safely home. Dan belonged to John, also known locally as Juan Coyote, who lived across the logging road at the foot of our trail. Dan was a cantankerous fellow but for some reason Julie could handle him. When she and the horse arrived, she was tired and tethered Dan to the railing near the cookshack. Fred greeted her, pleased at her accomplishment. We gathered around to quickly hear a short version of her adventure, then she headed to the cookshack for a well-deserved late lunch and cup of tea. I imagined that Julie would rest for the remainder of the day—and I encouraged her to do so.

*Camelsfoot's two horses.*

Meanwhile, Fred had gone over to stroke Dan's muzzle. He called me over as he untied the horse. He handed me the reins and told me to mount the beast. My big chance had arrived. I was thrilled — but what did Fred want me to do? I got into the saddle, feet in the stirrups, hands gripping the reins but not too tight. I knew a little bit about what I was doing, and I called on all my inner confidence.

"I want you to ride that horse hard. Take him up the pass and ride him like you would if you were just about to kill him," Fred instructed.

I wasn't at all sure what Fred meant. My romantic imagination conjured up an indigenous woman in buckskin with a knife strapped to her side, a vision no doubt gleaned from Willie's books. I liked this image quite a lot, though I knew I could never kill a horse, let alone much else. Fred probably wanted me to tire the horse out, and I didn't want him to think I hadn't a clue so I took Dan up the hill and into the meadow. Fred's scenario was under my skin. I clicked my tongue and flicked the reins back and forth over Dan's neck and haunches, digging my heels into his sides at the same time. The horse instantly broke into a gallop. I gripped the reins fiercely and hung onto his girth with every ounce of muscle in my thighs. This was so much fun! The message Fred put into me was working. I felt strong. In charge. Free.

» » »

As the weather got colder, working outside on our little pole cabin got more and more difficult. We longed to be in it, with the little wood stove crackling and all our things around us — even our cats, whom we had brought with us. In spite of the warm welcome of the others, we still wanted our own space. This need of ours, sometimes scoffed at by others, couldn't be helped. Our little family was used to being together, and we didn't want that to suddenly change. With four of us now sleeping in one tipi and Julie in her own tipi, our little family had no private place to just hang out together.

Living collectively, as we did on the commune, meant that we were always "on" — always trying to manoeuvre in a developing relationship with someone or someones whom we really didn't know yet (in the full-blown domestic way that we knew our own family). On occasion, the five of us would go down the trail and spend a night or two at a neighbour's place in the valley while the owners were away for a few days. We lounged around together on couches and beds and felt so relieved to have our own space, even if just temporarily. It turned out that even with the never-ending issues that a family can have, at least we were familiar, "at home," with one another. Making it up as we went along, as we had agreed to do at Camelsfoot, constantly required extra effort, and was often confusing and sometimes upsetting. It was not quite home yet.

That first winter was challenging. Some things grew more settled and known but others became increasingly complex and confusing. Our little family of five was finding its way. Shannon was sometimes happy and in the long quiet hours of winter had made some outstanding artwork. She used the ovoid technique of the indigenous peoples of the Pacific Northwest to create portraits of the Yalakom Yappers (the Cuban bear dogs), which delighted everyone. Occasionally she would pick up her saxophone.

*I was developing a sense of pessimism*

Willie was in heaven. Finally freed from the confines of his grade four desk, he grew his hair long and pulled it back with a leather thong, and with his small wool army pants was every day ready to cavort as much as possible in our chosen outdoor life. He learned so much.

Julie began a relationship with one of the communards that was not easy but took her "out." They travelled to northern California and met up with such luminaries as Peter Berg, Gary Snyder, Jim Dodge, and Freeman House, who taught them about Northern California's iteration of bioregionalism and sent them back with the news that we were not alone in our quest for community rooted in place. Julie joined the Green Party in British Columbia and took an active role in its early days.

Kip and I talked endlessly about what we thought we were doing in this adventure. He was optimistic about our experiment. I was developing a sense of pessimism as my familiarity with the group revealed deep divisions that I did not understand. But we carried on and made it to spring, when projects could be resumed and life would go on.

# SEVEN

# Work Hard, Play Hard, and Learn Lots

We were trying to give each one of us a well-rounded life on the commune. Some of us were very emphatic about this need; others, like me, were just grateful for any attention to the whole life experience. It would have been so easy for me to just work endlessly. All work and no play, they say, makes a dull person.

Once I twisted my ankle and had to rest with my foot up for a day or two. Eleanor brought me stacks of books and lots of tea. I started at the top of the pile and simply read. That evening she came into the cabin to chat with me, wondering what subject matter was filling my head. We talked and talked. At the end of our time together, she hugged me and said, "See, you need intellectual time. You're so interesting, given a chance." I knew what she was getting at, though we never talked about it explicitly. I had brought to the commune a real anxiety around responsibility. How could it be otherwise given my years of life as a single mother? And look at all the jobs there were to do . . .

So we organized ourselves to allow each of us to have a "day off." On your day, all your responsibilities were picked up by others. This was unusually formal for Camelsfoot, most likely because if we didn't do this deliberately, a day off simply wouldn't happen.

When my day came up it was a beautiful, hot summer day. Shannon and Willie were visiting their father in Ontario and Julie was away with a friend. Kip offered to cook dinner while covering listening hours on the radiophone. What a capable guy! My plan was to head up to Independence Ridge, with a lunch and my water bottle, and frolic in the mountains all by myself. I could hardly wait. After breakfast, I loaded up my day pack with rye tack, cheese and trail mix. I was in shorts and a T-shirt. With the precious Tilley hat that Eleanor had given me in hand and my stout hiking boots on my feet, I set off.

It took me a good hour to reach Independence Ridge, so named by Fred because from it one could access secret valleys where Fred said we could hide out if the shit ever hit the fan. I wasn't sure what, exactly, Fred was afraid of, but I loved the place. The mountain country was perfect for hiking. While it was hot, the air was dry. The smell of ponderosa pine was everywhere, the sap oozing from the bark like sticky toffee. The sound of the cicadas pierced the air. From the Ridge, valleys folded one into the other. This place was heaven on earth.

After an hour or so of steady climbing, I reached the top and stopped to soak up the vista and have a little lunch. It was really hot. I was the only human being for as far as the eye could see. I took off my shorts and T-shirt, feeling the sun's warmth all over me. A sensual and spiritual experience all in one.

Being a human being though, I was curious. So I left my clothes and pack in a little heap, and headed down the slope into one of these hidden valleys, wondering if there was water at the bottom, or just . . . wondering, and wandering. *Better get back up to the top and start thinking about heading home,* I finally thought. So I headed up. When I reached the top, it wasn't the same ridge. Back down I went, and then up in another direction. Again, not the same place. The sun was falling lower in the sky. I'd been out in the mountains alone since mid-morning and now I was naked except for my boots and hat, and beginning to panic. For the last time, I headed up. At least from a higher vantage point, I might be able to get some bearings. I was trusting myself because I had to; there was only me here and time was running out.

I knew that the sun hit Goat Mountain, behind our little settlement, in a certain way at a certain time in the late afternoon. So that was my direction. I started walking towards the setting sun. There was no trail, and I had to head downhill because of the terrain. Thrashing through underbrush, I stuck to my crude directions. My arms and legs were getting seriously scratched and were bleeding, though I hardly noticed this as I carried on. Eventually, I broke through into the lower garden.

With great relief, I headed home and almost fell into the cookshack. Kip seemed to me to be handling a huge amount single-handedly: listening to the radio phone, chopping vegetables, and keeping an eye on the several boiling pots. I was confused, and slightly ashamed that I got lost—but utterly relieved to see him.

He helped me wash the blood off my legs and couldn't help but chuckle, which rankled me. That was it! I had to reclaim my dignity. I had to head back up to Independence Ridge right then and there to get my clothes and pack. But dinner was just about ready, Kip said. I didn't care.

I put some clothes on, grabbed a flashlight and set off. Something in me insisted on completing this day by tying up my own "loose ends." I reached the Ridge in record time. I couldn't help but linger just a minute to take in the breathtaking scene, the evening light on the trees, the warmth of the day still being held by the soil and the rocks. The smell of the forest and the night sounds were all around me. I had found a new confidence in myself in this place that was always here, even when I was not. I marvelled at its magnificence, its huge solid presence, and reminded myself, with some humility, that I was the ephemeral one, just passing through. I did well, I told myself. I used my head and didn't ever give up. I gathered up my things and quietly made my way down the hill. What a gift that day had been!

One day, Scotty asked Kip and me if either of us had ever tried "scree jumping." Never, we said. I hardly even knew what scree was. "Great, let's go tomorrow," said Scott. No doubt Scott was looking for a break from the endless power-from-water project that he and Bonnie Mae had commandeered and which sometimes left him feeling alone and burdened. So it was with a spirit of escape from our work and responsibilities that he, Bonnie Mae, Kip, myself, and Willie set off after breakfast the next day. We headed up towards Goat Mountain, a steep rock face that looked down on our settlement, with rubble-edged sidehills for skirts. It was so named because from down below, with the help of a telescope, we often spotted mountain goats making their way across the high craggy ledges on unbelievably precipitous trails that were only passable by sure-footed goats. As we made our way through the ponderosas and the Douglas fir, Scott told us to look for sturdy poles, at least six feet tall for the adults.

It wasn't long before we realized we were sharing the forest with two big, "chocolate" brown bears. I had encountered bears before, mostly black ones in northern Ontario while picking blueberries, and never had any trouble, though that could have been the folly of my younger self. These bears, though not grizzlies, were huge animals. They turned and looked towards us. Of course they knew we were here. We stopped, made no eye contact, and the bears lumbered away. Already it had been an exciting day!

Up we went until we were above the tree line. We had

*Scott lets loose into the ecstasy of the heights.*

approached the top by walking in switchbacks, zig-zagging our way up. It was a much easier way to climb a steep slope than simply heading straight up, which in this terrain would have been impossible. By now we all had our poles and were using them as walking sticks, which helped stabilize us as we moved across the soft scree. It was a steep slope, and it was a long way down.

"Okay," said Scott, barely able to contain his enthusiasm. "It's taken us an hour and a half to get up here, and it's going to take us fifteen minutes to get down. I'll show you how it's done. Ready?"

Before we could reply, he was off. One foot after another sunk into the hillside and his body leaned back until it was parallel with the slope of the hill, and the pole became almost a "third leg" for balance. There was no stopping because the momentum gained from the intense steepness just kept pushing the "jumper" down the hill. It looked a bit like skiing but not quite; we were going downhill but on scree, which is quite different from powdery snow. Scott was yelping with delight. One at a time, we set ourselves free and scree jumped down the hill, letting loose into an ecstasy of the heights. It was incredible fun. Once down, we wanted to head straight back up the hill to try it again. No more time today. But we promised ourselves more of this fun later.

» » »

In early spring, Gordon returned to resume work on the water line. While his big machine was on-site at Camelsfoot, we asked him, once again, to do a few other "little" projects. The triple-seater outhouse hole he dug had saved us weeks of shovelling. This time we asked him to dig out two large water reservoirs at the top of the meadow, one larger than the other. We wanted to make the big one into a swimming hole, something we felt we almost needed. Summers were hot and the nearest lakes were alpine lakes, far from us and frigid. There was no doubt about it, the commune was excited. It was easy to imagine diving into a large swimming hole, even a

*Gordon digs the swim-*
*ming hole while some*
*communards watch.*

small lake, having real fun on days off with picnics, or even just taking a quick dip after a hot day. Susan had already designed a sauna to be built close by.

Gordon dug both reservoirs with his machine in a couple of days. On the edges, we bedded in a large eight-inch intake pipe and a similar overflow pipe so we could keep the water fresh and clean. What we hadn't managed to figure out was how the water would stay in the massive eight-foot-deep hole, how it could be kept from constantly draining out through the porous ground. Bonnie Mae and Scott scratched their heads in the evening, pondering the problem, and finally Bonnie Mae came up with an idea.

"We have rolls of heavy black plastic left over from the pipe-line," she said. "I think we can line the hole with it, and seal the edges together."

*Ironing the plastic . . .*
*it took a bunch of us.*
*Bonnie Mae irons*
*with Judith and Julie*
*helping, while Van*
*holds the cord and*
*others watch.*

"How, Bon?" asked Scott.

"With the iron. We'll take the portable generator up to the meadow, set up a huge 'ironing board' made from a couple of sheets of plywood on the sawhorses, and then iron the hundred-foot sheets together."

This sounded like a plan. It was bound to work.

I didn't know why, but it seemed to take all of us to do this job. I think now that it was so outrageous no one wanted to miss a moment of it, and the collective anticipation about sunny days "by the lake" spurred us on. Bonnie Mae set up her ironing board, down at the bottom of this huge hole with massive long and wide sheets of heavy black plastic, generator humming. With someone's old iron in hand, she ironed away, sealing the edges together. It was not as easy it sounds. She had to adapt the ironing process with feed sacks on top of the plastic so that the iron didn't get gummed up. Nevertheless, she carried on for hours. Meanwhile, the kids had brought planks and boards and set up a diving board, getting ready for their first swim.

The next day, with all the plastic in place and heavy logs around the perimeter holding the edges securely in place, it was time to fill it up. Someone opened the big valve, and water gushed out. Of course, it was freezing cold. In fact, it was frigid! We needed to let the sun heat it up for a few days before plunging in. After twenty-four hours and with great anticipation, several of us headed up the hill to check the water level. Our dreams were quickly crushed! The plastic was on top of the water, floating like a massive broken balloon, and the water was going down seemingly faster than it was coming in.

"Quick," Scott said, "turn it off. The whole thing is going to slough in. This is a disaster!"

True, but it sure was *fun* . . . while it lasted.

» » »

Fred told us from his sick bed that we had to keep the deer away from the meadow so that the horses could have all of the alfalfa. Camelsfoot is in the middle of the wilderness. We, and our critters, are the newly arrived; the deer have been here since, well, the beginning. We knew about the necessity of fences and enclosed spaces, having had a few encounters with the wild gods of the place, like bobcats, hawks, and cougars, who would like nothing better than to feast on our chickens. We were the domesticated and had to fence ourselves in, leaving the wilderness as the range of the wild ones. But how could we protect an expanse of territory like the meadow, the upper garden, and the hillsides that surround it all? It was vast.

"Drift fences," Fred said. "Take a crew, the fencing tool, rolls of wire, some rebar, and some wooden posts, and string it across the hillside high up above the Philosophers' Grove." A drift fence doesn't fence in, like the chicken coop, it just discourages the deer,

*Alice, Eleanor, and*
*Van work to fence in*
*the new garden site.*

taking them up high beyond the alfalfa, making it too much effort to get at the meadow. Perhaps they would even forget about the tasty grazing below.

So about six of us headed up with all the tools and equipment, a round of rye tack, and several cans of sardines. It was going to be an all-day effort. None of us had ever built a drift fence before, but we had a degree of confidence, having talked at length with Fred about the project. First, we had to dig post-holes. We were on a steep slope so the work was hard. Taking turns, we managed to dig in several dozen pieces of rebar, intermingled with the posts, all about ten feet or so apart. Next, with fencing staples, we attached the wire to the wooden uprights in three strands. With the fencing tool we tightened the lines, then hung colourful flags on the wire every eight feet or so.

I supposed that real cowhands would do this job all by them-selves. I couldn't imagine doing this with anyfewer than six people; I had to take frequent rests from the hot and heavy work. At lunch

I discovered that sardines squashed over rye tack was absolutely delicious. Never before would I have eaten such a fishy mess, but today it tasted great, especially with a little Indian pickle. And we had to have tea, which required a little fire to heat up water. And, of course, the habitual and endless conversation about who we are and what we're up to.

I thought about work and fun. Today's effort had been fun and hard work. This seemed right to me. True collegiality. I got excited thinking about what a group of people could accomplish together. With a playful attitude and good companionship, we could move mountains. Ever the entrepreneur, I thought that maybe we could even contract ourselves out. I thought we could do anything we set our collective minds to!

# EIGHT

# A Hard Lesson, and Real Love

It was March. We had been eating beans and rice alternated with mackerel curry for a long time. At night we talked about eating meat, fantasized about roasts and chops and ribs. We longed for heavy protein. The hillsides, of course, were full of meat, but all on the hoof. Only Fred had any hunting experience, and he could barely get out of bed.

Willie had been practicing with the .22, under Fred's careful watch, of course. He was developing a sharp eye, and he absolutely loved shooting. Earlier, in the late fall, the cookshack had been full of squirrels, and one in particular was driving everyone crazy. "Shoot it, would you Willie?" asked Van.

Taking him seriously, Willie did just that. He killed it instantly. It was a bit shocking for this young lad, the first time ending another critter's life. Afterwards, he didn't know what to do. I said, "Skin it out and we'll cook it. If you kill it, you have to eat it."

Really, I was thinking of the rest of us. I thought we all needed this lesson. I wanted us all to share some of the responsibility for taking the squirrel's life. Fortunately, there's not much meat on a squirrel, but we passed it around anyway.

So with this serious lesson in mind, Kip and Willie headed into the hills a few months later to look for a deer. Kip had never been hunting but he did know one end of a gun from another, and was a remarkably good shot given his lack of real-life experience. This will be an excellent bonding opportunity for my son and my new husband, I thought. Little did any of us know what was ahead of them. Had Kip known, he never would have attempted it. Of this I am absolutely certain.

I realized that neither Willie nor Kip would think about their long day as fun. No, I was quite sure as I looked at their faces when they walked slowly back home, that this had been anything but fun. I hoped they at least had an adventure and, as they told us their story, it was that and more.

They made a long story short, mostly I think because by the time they got home they were really upset. They had thrashed around in the bush for a long time and finally saw signs of deer. They followed, and sure enough they soon spotted one. Taking aim, one of them fired. The deer was hit in the shoulder but did not drop; rather it fled up the hill and deeper into the mountains. Even injured, a deer can move through the bush much easier than two-footed novices chasing it. It was really tough, they told us.

"But we had to find it because we'd injured it. We couldn't let it go off and die a miserable and painful death. We felt awful and this feeling just got worse and worse," said Kip. "We eventually caught up with the deer and finished it off with a single shot. Then, of course, we had to gut it so we could carry it back home." Their heads dropped, and their voices grew quiet. "Our hearts absolutely broke when we started to clean the animal. It was a doe, a pregnant doe."

I could only imagine that, at this point, the two of them were sobbing by the side of their kill. "I'm never going hunting again," said Willie. "Nor I," added Kip. "But here's the meat." We all had to eat it. With gratitude.

A hard lesson, but also a serious bonding, life-changing experience.

We told ourselves at Camelsfoot that people who have real culture, people whose culture embeds them in the landscape that feeds and nurtures them, have lots of holidays and reasons for getting together with song and dance and good food, probably all centered around cyclical natural events like equinox and solstice. Christmas, of course, was abandoned at Camelsfoot, though winter solstice shared some of the traditional elements, like bringing a tree inside and decorating it with homemade ornaments and beautiful little candles in tiny holders imported from Germany. There was a gift exchange, too, but the gifts were often things we already owned and were ready to pass on. Our story was that the tree and the gifts were pagan traditions from earth-centered celebrations around the darkest time of the year, which were appropriated by Christians. We were now reclaiming them!

If I'd had my way, we would have celebrated every night. I love good meals with friends, I love tea and dessert, I love homemade music and dancing. Kip quietly told me that we couldn't have a party every night. In some ways, though, quiet evenings together were like a small party, when we shared our thoughts, told our stories, or read aloud pithy gems from books, personal writing, or letters from friends There were so many of us that it was always interesting one way or another. Birthdays were another excuse for a shindig, and with sixteen of us, we had lots of those. Frequently, too, we were hosting friends or relatives who had come up the trail for a visit and who rarely went back down the same day. Camelsfoot had an active social life, and this worked well for my personality.

Much to my daughters' disdain, however, we had no recorded music at Camelsfoot: no records or tapes, and radios were impossible given our location. We had convinced ourselves that recorded music not only inhibited our own musical efforts, but brought the rejected mainstream world into our lives. This was not at all understood by my daughters, and caused them some resentment.

We did have two pianos, a violin, an accordion, two tea-box basses, endless recorders, at least three drums, Shannon's alto sax, a couple of flutes, and a grab bag of percussion instruments. Van was an accomplished jazz pianist, and almost refused to use sheet music. Susan and I had brought stacks of music books to the library, and, being an able sight reader, it had been a joy for me to go through her music. I especially liked the folk songs. But our homemade music pushed all of that organized music aside. Van usually set the rhythm (which sometimes was difficult for me to find) and a drummer would pick it out, and somehow something rambunctious emerged, something musical enough to set the youngsters dancing. Everyone could participate with some instrument or another. It was exciting to us all. Well, the teenagers weren't that thrilled but it was, most likely, better than listening to the endless drone of our boring adult conversation.

*Somehow something rambunctious emerged, something musical*

These sorts of musical moments — with accompanying dessert of applesauce, yogurt and tea — paled in comparison to the music and feasting of the big solstice celebrations. These gatherings included the wider community: friends of the commune, and our neighbours in the valley below us. When we hosted the winter solstice we had overnight guests for almost a week. It was a good experience for everyone, especially for Fred, who wouldn't have been able to make it had the event been elsewhere. In the brilliant cold and dark nights, with big fires to gather around, children everywhere, and great food, the celebrations seemed endless.

Our first summer solstice at Camelsfoot, most of us headed down the valley to a neighbour's homestead; they were hosting a gathering of about 100 neighbours and friends from far and wide. We couldn't all go, of course. Some had to stay home to take care of the place, especially all of the animals. Shannon took her alto sax along and Fraser, the valley's extraordinary soprano sax player, hoped that she would play with him. Shannon was a good musician too, but she was shy. Fraser was a big guy, in more ways than one, and could be a little intimidating, though I knew he didn't mean to discourage Shannon, or anyone. Her music has a way of touching the heart and has been known to move people to tears. I was very proud of her and hoped she'd feel comfortable enough to play for us all. She left Camelsfoot a few days early, with a couple of other folks, to help set up the event.

It was a Friday-to-Sunday celebration. I was going on Saturday night, which was the peak evening for the whole weekend. This was the night that no one wanted to miss. There was music until early Sunday morning, and a feast that took six or more long tables to present. Being summertime, the whole event took place outside. I arrived around 4:30 in the afternoon. Shannon was very busy in the outdoor kitchen so Kip and I set up our tent and got ready for the long night of partying. Around 7:30 we returned to the scene.

The food, all of the best and finest dishes contributed from everyone's kitchens, was beautifully laid out in the midst of bouquets of flowers, over Indian-print tablecloths. Candles were lit. I spotted Shannon behind Camelsfoot's contribution to the table: the largest ham I had ever seen. Of course, it was one of "ours," one of the precious pieces of meat that we had smoked in the old outhouse. Shannon was slicing the ham, carefully and skillfully. She looked up and saw me.

"Mom, come over here. I have a very special piece for you."

Shannon knew such a morsel would mean a great deal to me. We had known this animal, had taken its life, and now had the honour of sharing the eating of its flesh, turning that simple act into an affirmation of love between two people. My heart doubled in size. I was so proud. We each had all that we needed. I didn't think that life could get any better.

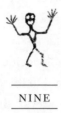

# NINE

# Power Outside and In...

It has to be said that not all of our families on the "outside" agreed with what we were up to. While some of our parents did — especially Scott's, who visited frequently and were very supportive and lots of fun to be with — most either reluctantly tolerated what their adult children were up to, or, I suspect, were patiently waiting for the whole thing to collapse so their children could get on with their "real" lives.

Kip's parents, much later, told me that they thought they'd lost him. They couldn't understand his rationalizations, didn't like the way he looked and dressed, and were very concerned for his future. The same thing could be said for my mother, though she was highly distracted by my younger sister, who became very ill during this period and needed her attention far more than I did.

Bonnie Mae and I, however, had serious issues with the fathers of our respective children. Bonnie Mae's troubles happened prior to our family's arrival at Camelsfoot, and we drew on her experience when my turn came to deal with my children's irate father. He had remarried several years prior and he and his growing new family lived in Ontario. Theirs was a village life, full of the richness that a small community affords. I have since come to appreciate the value of the many summers my three children spent there with their father. However, when I quit my job, took the children out of school, and moved to Camelsfoot, and, as my ex-husband later said publicly through his lawyer, became a "dirt farmer," the gap between our chosen lifestyles became a massive chasm, and led to a severe lack of understanding.

When summer arrived Julie decide not to go, but Shannon and Willie, as they always did, went to their father's for their scheduled four week visit. This time, however, they did not return. Instead I was ordered to show up in a courtroom in Ottawa to answer charges heaped on me by their father and the state. With a lot of support from Alice's mother in Toronto and my uncle in Ottawa, Kip and I and Julie travelled to Ontario, quietly found the children at their school yards, and took them off for a weekend of family time together. If they wanted to stay with their dad, I would not get in the way. But, I felt, such a decision had to be made with me.

Meanwhile, back at Camelsfoot, the RCMP had driven over the seven-mile mountain pass that culminated in the beautiful Camelsfoot meadow. Taking the children from their schools had triggered an all-points bulletin for me. When the police arrived they discovered the communards naked but for their hats and boots, doing what they loved to do most: sunbathing with their books and each other. Van, always charming, walked up to the big four-by-four before the cops even got out of the car. With his floppy hat and well-mannered ways, he leaned on the window frame and assured the officers that he had no idea where I, or the children, could be. He was convincing enough that they turned around and headed back over the pass without ever getting out of their vehicle.

But the power of the state was seriously breathing down my neck. The world we had rejected didn't have much flexibility when it came to the well-being of children. After what I later considered to be the speech of my life in a small anteroom outside the courtroom, the judge gave me three months to prove that my son could tell time, and that he was receiving an education. And he wanted this proof from a professional child psychologist.

Shannon told me honestly that she wanted to be with her father.

I was not surprised, knowing that she had been disgruntled from the outset. With some sadness but also some relief we dropped her off at her dad's place and headed home.

Bonnie Mae gave me the name of a child psychologist, whom I hired immediately. She agreed to assess my son in two and a half months' time. With great enthusiasm, everyone on the commune rallied around this project. Willie delighted in being the centre of attention. He loved to learn and absorbed everything we put before him. We were, after all, a group of over-educated intellectuals with a variety of interests. It was a pleasure to share ourselves with the children. Books, learning, conversation . . . this is what this collection of people was all about. We were constantly trying to place our social experiment in historical, indeed evolutionary terms.

*The contrast between 'ourselves' and 'them' deepened*

Three months later, after Willie had taken many tests and gone through many interviews, we received a copy of the report that had been sent to the court in Ontario. Willie, the psychologist said, was one of the loveliest children she had ever met. At age eleven, he read at a grade twelve level. His math skills were developed way beyond the academic requirement for his years. More than this, though, she wrote, he was an interesting person, happy, and well-adjusted.

So ended that power struggle. For now. "Power-over" from the outside, though, was always lurking. I never fully recovered. The contrast between "ourselves" and "them" deepened. There was a magazine on the grocery store shelves titled *Us*; Scott jokingly called it *Them*. This said it all. We were giving our life experience to the project of creating an alternative to the marketplace, to the frightening world of the individual in a society bent on keeping us separate through commerce — and, as it turned out, the law.

Power-over did not just come from "out there." Back at the ranch we had our own structural issues. It was not clear to me who was the boss. Of course, there wasn't supposed to be a boss. If there had been a clear-cut boss, we'd have had many fewer tense, uncertain moments. If we were Christians, for example, and our leader was a direct descendant of God, things would have been much easier. We would have known who was in charge.

Being a feminist, I had found, was often very trying, in a similar sort of way. If only my role as a conscious woman were understood — if only I knew what to do, how to do it, who to do it with and why. But no, I had to be constantly thinking, analyzing, figuring it out.

*We told ourselves there wasn't a hierarchy at Camelsfoot, but I saw that there was*

It was much the same on the commune. With no compass and no chart, as Fred liked to say, social organization was very murky. We were all supposed to be in charge. If only we could wake up in the morning to a written page telling us where to go and what to do, with a little affirmation in italics at the top of the page as a reminder of who we are and why we're here, just to make things perfectly clear . . . life together would have been a piece of cake! Alas, that was not the case. Which is why we sat in the Adirondack chairs for hours and hours and hours.

All of us, I'm sure, would have liked to know from the beginning what to do, and then we would have happily gotten on with it. Oh, of course, as long as what we were doing was what we wanted to do; as long as our projects, for example, took precedence. Circular madness. The individual and the common weal . . . difficult territory. How do highly educated individuals with varying degrees of attitudes of entitlement and yes, privilege, put themselves aside enough to be able to think clearly and creatively on behalf of the whole? It might have sounded simple, but then personalities arose like looming dragons.

Weapons of words emerged from everyone, sometimes in the form of long rants, more often in snide hurtful comments. People took sides on goats versus cows, horses versus tractors, and other issues that came up and never went away. Judgments about each other flew around the cookshack like whirling devils, keeping destructive company with all the doubts we brought with us from our own backgrounds of class and privilege. A passive aggressive battle all about power and control simmered just below the boiling point.

I was a newcomer here, and even I had developed a few issues of my own, but most of these folks had been living together for several years in Vancouver before our family emerged on the scene. I knew there was a history, that there were deep issues. But I couldn't quite get a handle on what exactly was at issue. Was it about the goats? Or the proposed site of the big garden? Or the hundreds of fruit trees? Or the money? Or who was sleeping with whom? What was getting under people's skins? If it was about goats or cows, then we could have looked at the pros and cons. But no, this didn't work. Sides were entrenched, there was no budging, and the more almost any topic came up, the worse it seemed to get. In the midst of all of this, I felt that I could not bring up my own issues. Whether I cooked dinner or not seemed trivial. But there were other larger, uncertain and uncomfortable things going on for me, too.

We told ourselves there wasn't a hierarchy at Camelsfoot. But I saw that there was. Everyone loved and respected Fred, but some folks were closer to him than others. Some had his ear in a different way. Others strived for that. Some were men, some were women. Or, I asked myself, was what I saw a projection of my own issues? Kip thought there were class issues, some of us having had a privileged upbringing, others more of a working-class background. There was no denying that the world we were trying to reject was mean and cruel. None of us, without exception, wanted to repeat these cruelties in our new world. And yet . . . my head broke from the effort of trying to grasp Camelsfoot's "big picture."

As Fred got sicker and sicker he grew more and more feisty. He was irritable, short-tempered. But then he was in pain most of the time and was slowly starving to death. It was tough for everyone watching this man decline before our very eyes as he struggled to keep up with life around him. He came out of his room in the evenings, and with Susan's care and attention, settled into his recliner next to the big wood stove. Often he kept his toque on, his wool cardigan over his robe, a big blanket over his knees. A cup of instant coffee was never far from his reach. He had always been in the centre of everything, not the least of which were the evening conversation circles. Sometimes he would attempt to share his scholarly readings with us, and occasionally he inserted generalized comments about our social situation that almost always went over my head. Though the positions he held on our unraveling micro-society must have been discussed in private with Susan and perhaps also with Van, to my recollection he never addressed our divisions directly, nor did he discuss with the rest of us the part that he undoubtedly played in the whole scheme of things.

Once in a while he got up during the day and, fully dressed, headed out into the barnyard. He was not just a man of words but also a man who loved to do things. It must have pained him greatly to be so debilitated with disease. And he had skills that the rest of us sorely lacked. He knew about living in the bush from a lifetime of experience. He wanted to participate in the work of the chainsaw, the horses, and the goats. But the never-ending internal contradiction between wellness and illness, this struggle that he was losing . . . was this why he was dismissive of the rants and seemed to hardly notice, if at all, the short tempers of others? I got the feeling that Fred knew how things should be and that the rest of us just had to come to terms with his "rightness."

This unspoken cloud lingered over the commune. This was not what we were supposed to be all about. When Kip and I joined the commune we thought we were entering into a more flexible situation, where everyone was equal and had a real say in how things were to evolve. The more Fred fixed his position on any one issue, the more resistance there seemed to be. Tensions mounted. I saw sides taking shape, folks digging their heels in, positions lining up.

I sensed the strain and stress every day. Kip and I waffled on whose side to take. Sometimes we heard people say that because of who were we would side with those who appeared less powerful, the underdogs. But I felt myself drawn to the others. Did I think it would be safer there? What was all this about? Self-doubt crept in.

In retrospect, I see now that some things are bigger than any one of us, or even two or three of us. Power, pure power was expressing itself in our need to control each other. This, more than any specific issue, was our bête noire. We were relentless in our persistence to resolve our entangled relationships, yet people never budged. The knots we were in would not release just because of Fred's frustrations. I was gradually understanding that Fred refused to see his position in the whole scheme of things. He would not acknowledge his part, how his attitude was contributing to a larger mess.

*Fred pulled himself out of the chair, energized by a fit of rage*

One morning things reached a head. Van asked all the adults to gather in the cabin to witness whatever would be said, and to add our two cents. Van was standing, his face drawn and forlorn, and Fred was in his chair. I was next to Fred on the couch. Van was taking Fred to task. Power was having its way with us. I tried to say something but my remarks seemed out of place. Bigger things were going on. I felt myself starting to smile, and I had no idea why. I hoped that no one noticed.

The details of whatever the issue at hand was have long since faded in my memory. What remains in my mind's eye is how courageous Van was in questioning his mentor, his long-time teacher, his guide in this new world, indeed, his senior. Fred pulled himself out of the chair, energized by a fit of rage. He headed to the door of the cabin and took himself outside. Before any of us could do or say anything, he had mounted the saddled horse that was tethered by the cookshack. In a flash of hooves Fred was gone. And we were left. Alone. Sad and bereft.

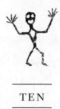

# TEN

# We Lose Fred... Forever

In the second fall since my family's arrival, during Fred's last days, his youngest daughter Heide arrived with her children for a visit. Fred enjoyed her company. Heide and the kids stayed a couple of days. It was hard for her because Fred was so sick, and Heide must have known that this might be the last time she would be with her father. The morning of her departure, Fred got out of bed to see her off. As she and her family headed up the road, away from the cabin, Fred was at the big picture window waving goodbye. It was a poignant moment for everyone.

After Heide was well on her way, Fred went back to bed and very soon after had a stroke and lost consciousness. Susan seemed to know what to do. We took turns rubbing his feet to keep the circulation going while she stayed at the head of his bed. This went on for hours. During the night Julie took over massaging Fred's feet and suggested that Susan take a break. Suddenly Fred sat up and seemed to look Julie in the eye. Julie called to Susan, and by the time Susan realized what was happening, Fred had once again fallen back on the bed, unconscious. In the morning nothing had changed.

We decided that Fred should go to the hospital. But how to get him there? We called for an ambulance to meet us on the other side of the pass, at our neighbour's place at the bottom of the road. Some of us prepared a bed in the back of Ike, and others carried Fred outside and loaded him with great care into the truck. I thought to myself that Fred would like this exit strategy.

The old friends drove him over the pass and met the ambulance. They all headed to town, thirty kilometres away. Once Fred was in the hands of the docs at the hospital, the others got a motel close by. The next day we got the phone call. The few of us left behind, back at the commune, gathered around the radio telephone in the cookshack to hear every word. Fred had died.

We hardly knew what to say, as is often the case in these situations. Of course we knew that Fred's death was coming but who is ever really prepared? Willie was especially distraught. Standing in the cookshack looking towards me, he tried not to cry but cried anyway; he was inconsolable. He had lost a really good friend, teacher, and grandfather. None of us knew what to do with ourselves.

But, there was always work to do, and so we set about making sure everything would be in order when our friends returned. This is a great part of community. Many hands and hearts work well together when crisis strikes. I think our true nature is revealed in such moments. The work helped everyone to know they had a part to play in keeping things going, and going well. There was a "temporary ceasefire" on all issues. At this moment, it all seemed petty to me anyway. A man we loved and respected had died.

When things got real, we rallied. There was still an ominous tension just below the surface, but we rose above it and took care of those closest to Fred — and ourselves. We did this with grace and equanimity. We behaved. We did the best that we could for each other. It was only later, with the luxury of time, that we once again lost our collective grip and things started to crumble. And when this happened no one behaved well. No one.

Susan was stricken with grief. A week or so after she and friends returned, Susan took me aside and said, "We are both grieving a loss. I have lost Fred and you have lost a child." I comforted her with my agreement because it was easier than discussing our issues, but we were not in the same position. Shannon was not gone forever.

Over the next few months things got really messy. I realized that Fred, even with his sickness and his impatience, had been the glue that held us together—even if the glue wasn't sticking all that well. What he left behind was a collection of broken hearts and vanished dreams, and the winter ahead looked long indeed. I don't recall many of the details but the emotional atmosphere I can easily remember. Fred left behind a deeply divided and ultimately untenable situation. It seemed that no matter the subject, lines were drawn with resentment, suspicion, and disrespect. Anger came to the surface, mixed with tears, some despair, and most definitely grief. In retrospect, I think we hardly knew what sorrow we were dealing with. Not only was Fred gone but our dreams seemed to go with him. No one was in the mood to try to reclaim our inspiration. Still, we turned to each other in small groups hoping for some fresh brand of sanity, some insight into how to proceed. This most likely only fragmented us even further but how were we to know? At every turn, our efforts seemed vacuous. We were all caught in a downward spiral of confusion and despair that was out of our control.

*All around were the ruins of our beautiful life together.*

During the early weeks and months after Fred's death, Kip and I made several trips to Vancouver, sometimes with the kids and sometimes without. Sometimes we went to Victoria, where Kip had political friends we could visit. We tried to talk about something else, tried to turn our minds away from our troubles. Yet everywhere we went people were very curious about what happened to our commune. We told our story. It was so damn serious to us. Most folks wanted to know the details of who said what about whom. We tried to tell them, if only in an effort to get a grip on our situation. There was a certain "I told you so" response. What else could be expected from human beings? From what our friends knew, the whole idea was folly from the beginning .

Our inspiration had died. We couldn't summon it up anymore. We couldn't defend our beautiful dream of community to anyone — most importantly, not even to ourselves. I cried every day for a long time. Kip and I almost split up. My mother offered us sanctuary in her home in Cape Breton. I thought about outrageous ideas like going to law school. I was grasping at straws. We were crushed.

Kip and I made the tough decision about a year after Fred's death to leave the commune. None of it made any sense to us. We couldn't figure out how to be useful. And there was a certain desperation that I felt about my own life, my own ambitions, and what could be salvaged, if anything. I had worked so hard to get myself through university only to find my life now in shreds. I was not angry, but I was despondent and frightened. I felt like a loser, like I was leaving behind my regard for "the whole" and once again taking refuge in the self.

Julie and her new boyfriend had returned from traveling and, seeing the confusion at Camelsfoot, decided to set up a small household for themselves in the valley rather than return to the Foot. They offered Kip and I and Willie a home with them, though there wasn't really space for us all. Luckily a little cabin at the foot of the Camelsfoot trail came up for sale. Together the four adults scraped up the down payment and made a deal for the place. It was not far away from the dear friends we were abandoning, we told ourselves. We felt guilty, but this close proximity made us feel a bit better, as if maybe with a little distance we could salvage something of what had been lost.

So now there were fewer folks at Camelsfoot. And all around were the ruins of our beautiful life together. Kip and I and our children had come into this "new world" in the middle of turmoil. We saw this now. And we could leave. We did not own the property, our names had not been added to the title. The place, ultimately, was not our responsibility. We could just turn our backs on the suffering and walk down the trail.

Others, however, couldn't just leave, and I knew that those folks were the ones suffering the most. Not only were they legally connected to Camelsfoot, they were also morally responsible for Susan, who was still deeply grieving. Those who remained were seriously divided. With the five of us out of the picture, there was less contextual cushion for the polarized relationships; everyone was forced to take a stark either/or position. A completely intolerable situation.

One day about a month after we moved into our new collective household, we looked from our new vantage point across the gulch to where the Camelsfoot trail ended. We saw three people — Bonnie Mae, Scott, and Alannah — carrying heavy packs and walking at an almost dirge-like pace towards their parked vehicle. Their heads were bent forward and they appeared to be almost dragging their feet. More people leaving. I was so upset. This meant that only the three closest friends of Fred remained at Camelsfoot: Susan, Eleanor and Van, and, of course, four-year-old Robin. That was it. And they couldn't just stay home and recover, loving and caring for each other. No. They didn't get along either, and now had to face each other and their own issues. It seemed heartless to leave them so alone, but we were of no help at all. At that moment we were helpless *and* hopeless.

What had happened to us? Where did it go wrong? What could we have done? What *should* we have done? What we built together had seemed so right, so authentic, so much of our own making, so important in the whole scheme of things, so vibrant. Our lives were in our own hands. It was so thrilling that we were blinded to the trajectory of our own downfall. "We have met the enemy, and it is us," said Pogo, the Walt Kelly comic strip character. We could not see this, so dazzled were we by our own inspiration, the swelling of our potential power and abilities.

Fred was a generation or two older than the rest of us, and had attempted intentional community a number of times. His experience was a gift to the rest of us. He played a key role, yet during all of my time at Camelsfoot he was very sick. People who are looking death in the face lose patience with endless bickering. Sometimes there was little room for others — in an odd way, since we were "in community" — and I'm not sure that Fred ever really understood the impact of his power and how it got in the way. Even if he had been more self-aware, had had the ability to achieve the high degree of self-consciousness required to set himself aside enough to let others in, I'm not sure it would have made any difference. There was still the rest of us and all our issues.

Van always said that to be able to truly join the commune one first had to be completely demoralized by western civilization. Kip and I could never accept this. Van was right in theory, but as far as I could tell, not in reality. We were all competent and capable people, and some of us were successful before our time on the commune. None of us were demoralized. We were naive. Maybe I didn't understand, but Kip and I felt ourselves to be the opposite of demoralized. We were inspired by the others, convinced that together we could change the world with the very actions of our lives.

*A Camelsfoot tipi at night.*

We told ourselves that we were no longer welcome in mainstream society. The communards might have felt rejected by the establishment, but to my mind it was us doing the rejecting. I saw us as renegades who chose to step outside of the system. By choice we donned the cloak of demoralization. It became a superman cloak, dipped in our story of community that we told each other almost daily. This story gave us the framework and the power we needed to convince ourselves that we were living outside of society's expectations, that we had created something new. Little did we know that this cloak couldn't protect us from ourselves. A thin veil, indeed, was this convincing cloak. When the persistent self inevitably pushed through our protective gear, we were forced to confront our tattered collective story and our shattered egos. Now I did feel demoralized.

I saw that all of us at Camelsfoot — every one of us, without exception — were children of western civilization, with more attitudes of entitlement and privilege and feelings of fear and insecurity than anyone could shake a stick at. For hundreds of years, through the generations, "the people" have been undermined. The litany of cruelty and greed is long indeed. Some might say that it began with the Enclosures Act in England in the twelfth century, when ordinary people lost the Commons; others might point to residential schools, where culture was brutally stripped away not so long ago. My reading of history tells me that we have been robbed in many ways, and I don't know if it will ever end. This, in my experience, is the stuff that keeps us apart. It was far from natural for us to live in isolation like machine parts. We were social creatures who had been blown apart.

In spite of all this, at Camelsfoot we found something precious and vital in ourselves, something that, unless nurtured to life, lies dormant in all of us like a frozen seed, a potential that sits waiting to germinate. This is why we yearn for a meaningful and caring life with others. This is our natural right and I will not, indeed I cannot, let it go. This knowing, for me, is the great legacy of our effort at Camelsfoot. Though never perfect, there were moments when our life together hummed within our own integrated society, and when life really made some social sense. Fragile moments, I see now, but real enough. As I looked across the creek to my friends leaving Camelsfoot, I steeled myself for the work of readjusting and getting back on my feet. I knew I would carry this gift with me forever. And I am still grateful for it.

# *Another World is Possible*

I still praise our audacity in thinking that we could actually create another world. What a noble dream! It's true that our vision of community, of a band of inquiring individuals homesteading on 160 acres in a secluded mountain valley, did not blossom as we had intended. Still, more than once, in fact, more often than we recognized at the time, we caught a glimpse of what it might be like to live in a caring, interesting and meaningful human community. This sense of belonging within a living culture, powered by the social romance of a coherent group of people around a common hearth—this, some say, is real love.

As it turned out, it couldn't possibly succeed. These glimpses of another world were fleeting, so absorbed were we in our issues and problems. Within our cherished, undivided life we had only ourselves to look at, day after day, with all of the desperate dysfunctions that we had inevitably carried with us up the trail and strewn about in a shambles of discord.

Van used to say to the nay-sayers, "You try it." I agreed, and added, "Give us a break." As late-twentieth-century lost souls, when it came to culture building, and a lot of other things, we were children, mere babes in the woods, with no coherent culture of our own and little notion of a sense of place. Entrenched in the ways of individualism, our baggage was loaded with assumptions, expectations, fears, and sometimes a complete lack of ability to understand each other. Even with our spirit of inquiry, and our determination to make it work, the cards were stacked against us. Our beautiful dream inexorably took a turn for the worse.

And so we split apart. One by one, we went in different directions. Some of the original communards still live in the Yalakom Valley. Others have moved on. In our individual ways we have made sure to keep in touch with each other, for once a common hearth is shared there is a deep connection that insists on being honoured.

While I can't speak definitively for anyone but myself, I would hazard a guess that each of us would say that the remainder of our lives have been influenced significantly by our attempt at community, by our shared "real love." All of us have spent the rest of our lives crafting community in our own ways, as educators, municipal activists, environmental activists, wordsmiths, academics, good parents, and seed-savers. The list goes on. All of us continue to contribute in meaningful ways to the worlds that we live in today. I know that I do the work that I do from the "knowing" that I discovered in the midst of our "failure," this truth about human beings, which once known can't ever be forgotten: community is part of our human nature. We need and want each other in our lives in a meaningful and caring way.

Three decades later, as the human condition continues to fragment and deteriorate, and the suffering of people and planet escalates, we need each other more than ever. The state of the world relentlessly breaks our human heart. We despair and wonder how much more can be endured. And yet suffering continues. We are a species blown apart, in serious trouble. As Fred said, we have lost the capacity to adapt to each other and the world in which we live, leaving us disorganized, and so we have been easy prey for the forces of separation and greed. There is no other sane response to the human crisis before us than to wake up and look to each other for another way.

Yes, another world is possible. But it's not simply a matter of protesting, of saying "no" to the old world and therefore "yes" to the new. And yes, the self-conscious social organization that Fred called for may be the greatest challenge our human community has ever faced. Without conscious, collective thought on how we are to be with each other, we are destined to re-create the same old patterns. There's no way around it. Creating a new world will not happen unless we are willing and able to recover from the old world — the false pretenses and privilege and all else that keeps us apart.

Can we find the passion and the patience it will take to prepare the ground for such a transformation? Can we muster up the courage to stand up and stay put long enough to build coherent, caring cultures of place? Are we ready to be free-thinking, self-determining people, grown-ups at last? Can we do this? Can we turn and face the dragon?

There's only one way to find out.

# Acknowledgements

Last winter, my first winter alone after Kip's passing in late June, this project was my solace. As the dark days went on and on, the writing conjured up a time and place full of hope and inspiration. I revelled in the memories and was reminded over and over again of the significance of the work that all of us did at Camelsfoot. I am proud of our effort, and still humbled by the enormity of the task we undertook. Thank you to Rolf Maurer for the idea and for approaching me at just the right time.

Special thanks goes to Van Andruss, dear friend, fellow communard, and life-long writer. I was nervous sending my early drafts to him. I needn't have been. He was unflinchingly supportive and respectful of my story.

As was Tschitschi, who would save my pieces for Sunday mornings with leisurely breakfast at his home in Freiberg. My stories took him back to those early days when he, too, was a companion and one of the dear friends who heard our endless tales from the commune. I thank him for his kind feedback and encouragement.

Eleanor Wright, close friend and fellow communard, read every word and offered her sharp editorial comments with love and support. We were sisters together in our Camelsfoot experience, and we're sisters today. I am grateful for her friendship.

Hattie Aitken, dear friend of almost four decades, I thank you for your time and effort over my pages and pages of words. She very carefully read every one, sometimes tidying up my rambling thoughts.

And to Rob West, thanks for taking the time to read. You are one busy fellow, and I appreciated your feedback and encouragement.

A good editor is a writer's best friend. I am lucky, indeed, that Betsy Nuse agreed to take on this project. Her gentleness and skill has polished my work. More than this, I feel that she is a kindred spirit. Thank you so much.

I couldn't have gotten through last winter without Julie, my eldest daughter, who read every word as I cranked it out. What pleasure it gave us to share these stories together. She was there at Camelsfoot. She's here now. Making my stories work for her was essential. Thank you, forever and ever.

My son Willie, whom you read about in these pages, also embraced the work, reading it at night to his partner Julia as it rolled off my computer. So meaningful for him to share this time of his life with his life partner. Couldn't be better. Thank you for your encouragement and for being there for me.

Shannon, my middle child, will read the work soon, in its finished form. Someone had to wait for this magical moment. It will be hers. Hope she likes it . . .

Copyright Judith Plant 2017. All rights reserved. No part of this work may be reproduced, stored in a retrieval system or transmitted, in any form or by any means, without the prior written consent of the publisher or a licence from the Canadian Copyright Licensing Agency (Access Copyright).

 NEW STAR BOOKS LTD.
newstarbooks.com • info@newstarbooks.com

#107–3477 Commercial St     1574 Gulf Road, #1517
Vancouver, BC     Point Roberts, WA
V5N 4E8 CANADA     98281 USA

The publisher acknowledges the financial support of the Canada Council for the Arts and the British Columbia Arts Council.

Cataloguing information for this book is available from Library and Archives Canada, collectionscanada.gc.ca

All photos by Kip Plant unless otherwise indicated
Cover by Rayola Creative
Typesetting by New Star Books
Printed & bound in Canada by Imprimerie Gauvin
First printing, May 2017